Great A
Motorcycle Tours
of the Northeast

Gary McKechnie

Contents

Advice from a Road Scholar

The more you ride, the more you learn. A few decades on the road and several thousand miles in the saddle have given me some insights that may improve the quality of your own ride.

Even if you're in a hurry to reach Point B, try not to leave Point A after mid-afternoon. Chances are you'll be racing the sun and you'll miss the moments you're riding for. If you leave in the morning, you'll have a full day to make unscheduled stops and discover points of interest.

Don't run a marathon. While you could ride 600 miles a day, 200 miles max is easy and allows for unexpected discoveries.

If you get off-schedule, don't worry. The purpose of touring isn't to reach as many places as possible, it is to experience as many sensations and places as you can. Don't kill yourself with a self-inflicted plan.

Reward yourself. Every so often, stop at a place you don't think looks very interesting at first. Take a break and meditate.

Watch what's going on around you. A conversation with a general store clerk, a swim in a pond, or the sight of glistening pebbles in a riverbed can be just as pleasing as a good stretch of road.

In general, the best times I've found for riding are May and September. Nowhere is it too hot or too cold, kids are still in or headed back to school, and few places are charging peak season prices.

Have a contingency plan in case your day gets rained out. Write postcards; see a museum or a movie; read, rest, or go to the library; talk to locals. If a day gets screwed up by weather, roll with it.

Carry a few sealable plastic bags. Somehow rain can find wallets and you might want to stow that and any small electronics inside.

If you use a magnetic tank bag, don't toss your wallet in it. The powerful magnets that can withstand 90-mile-an-hour winds can also demagnetize ATM and credit cards in a flash.

It can be maddening when a truck

ahead of you slows you down to its pace. If you pass, often the truck speeds up, and then you've got to worry about a tailgater. Instead, just pull over for a few minutes and take a break. It'll give the truck time to move on and allow you to return to scenic roads unobstructed by Yosemite Sam mud flaps.

It gets mighty cold when the sun goes down. Even if you don't think you'll need it, bring along long underwear.

If you can't avoid the small animal in front of you, grit your teeth and go for it. It's not worth laying down your bike to save a squirrel.

And remember that loose gravel, wet leaves, and oil slicks don't care how long you've been riding. Don't get so swept up in the ride that you neglect safety.

I hate paying banks three bucks to get my money from their ATMs. So I look for a drugstore (CVS, Walgreens, etc.), where I use my debit card for gum or candy or batteries and get cash back. Not only do I avoid a fee, I get something I want.

When I arrive in a town, before I check into a hotel or start walking around, I stop at the local chamber of commerce or visitors center and get maps and advice on hours, admission fees, and what's worth seeing. The staff know what's shakin', and they'll always have current information on back roads.

Don't forget alternative newspapers (usually free) and the Friday edition of most daily newspapers that include listings and reviews of local restaurants, concerts, and special events.

Ask nicely, and some local libraries may allow you to use their computers for free Internet access. Get online to check out upcoming towns, attractions, and seasonal operating hours, and to print out discount coupons if offered.

If you have to ride in peak tourist season, do your best to get up early and wander around the town. Minus the presence of other tourists, it reveals a more natural sense of the community.

A word about the lodging prices listed throughout this book: They are listed for peak seasons, but will vary by day and by month. If they seem to skew high, check their off-season rates and ask for a discount—AAA, AARP, AMA. To secure even better rates, visit websites like www. hotels.com or www.priceline.com. You can deduct approximately 10–15 percent if you're a solo traveler, and even more if you can travel in an off- or shoulder season. The same with admission prices—those are for adults and you can ask for a senior discount if you qualify.

If you plan to visit more than one national park, spring for the $80 America the Beautiful Pass (only $10 for ages 62 and older). It's good for admission to any national park for one year.

It's nice to wear full leathers and clothes that reflect the hard riding you've done, but use common sense and courtesy and dress appropriately when at certain restaurants.

Yes, the boots do make you look like Fonzie, but if you plan on joining any walking tours or beating your feet around a town, you'll appreciate the comfort of a pair of walking shoes.

Take wrong turns. Get lost. Make discoveries.

White Mountains—Blue Seas Run

Littleton, New Hampshire to Bar Harbor, Maine

From the mountains to the oceans white with foam, this run is relatively short, but with distinct changes in landscape and culture it actually feels quite large. Individually, the two legs described here offer experiences that are not breathtaking, but still enjoyable; a nice balance of mountain rides, coastal runs, and an opportunity to get off your bike and head out to sea. Note that many stores and restaurants—especially in Maine—close from mid-October to Memorial Day.

Also consider alternate routes and side trips that will add some horsepower to your ride—particularly down some of Maine's peninsulas. While I've included some options here, you're ever so welcome to add your own.

When you hit those rare long stretches of road, you'll have time to think. I thought about New Hampshire's license plates; the ones stamped with the state motto, Live Free or Die. It's appropriate, considering New Hampshire has no helmet law, no state sales tax, and no state income tax.

It's quite ironic, however, when you consider who's stamping out those tags.

LITTLETON PRIMER

At first glance, Littleton, New Hampshire, looks like a blue-collar town that never experienced a recession. A Main Street program has kept up the town's appearance, and the lack of a mall (amen!) brings many of its roughly 6,000 citizens downtown throughout the day. Equidistant from both Boston and Montreal (160 miles in either direction), Littleton is nestled in the Connecticut River Valley and sits at the doorstep of two great roads that sweep into the 780,000-acre White Mountain National Forest. This location alone makes it worth the ride.

Historically, Littleton has tended to stay in the shadows. Named after the region's surveyor, Colonel Moses Little, the town made its first contribution to American history during the Revolutionary era when unusually straight tree trunks around town were recycled as masts for sailing

7

White Mountains–Blue Seas Run

Route: Littleton to Camden via Mount Washington, Kancamagus Highway, Fryeburg, Yarmouth, Waldoboro, Thomaston

Distance: Approximately 280 miles

First Leg: Littleton, New Hampshire to Camden, Maine (210 miles)

Optional Second Leg: Camden to Bar Harbor, Maine (72 miles)

Helmet Laws: No helmets are required in New Hampshire or Maine.

ships. If you happen to be building a sailing ship, strap one of those mothers onto your handlebars and bolt.

About a century later, prior to the Civil War, Littleton was an essential stop on the Underground Railroad. If you're invited into some of the town's older homes, check out the basements where runaway slaves were shielded until they could continue their trek to Canada. At the turn of the 20th century, two companies—one manufacturing stereoscopic view cards and the other, gloves—did their part to keep the town in the black. Aside from those highlights, things stayed pretty quiet until an author ranked Littleton among his hundred favorite small towns and retirees and families started taking a second look at the place.

Now it's your turn.

ON THE ROAD: LITTLETON

When you arrive, you'll do so on Route 302 (Main Street) which barrels through the center of town, a fact that makes this unappealing for a leisurely cruise. Instead, take advantage of the cheap curbside parking—just drop a dime in the slot and you'll own that section of pavement for the next hour. Since Littleton isn't an upscale village, but a working town that happens to attract a handful of tourists, these bargain rates extend from parking meters into the restaurants, inns, and hotels. What's more, the town's independent merchants don't put on a show for your cash; they seem genuine and friendly.

Logistically, Littleton is a perfect starting point for a ride, since it's the largest town on the western end of Route 302 and also close to the Kancamagus Highway (112). Visually, the town seems locked in the 1950s. When night falls, you can just listen to the Ammonoosuc River flowing past, order a burger, fries, and a chocolate frappe at a Main Street diner, and then walk across the street to catch the evening picture show. Simple pleasures in a pleasant town.

PULL IT OVER: LITTLETON HIGHLIGHTS
Attractions and Adventures

The Littleton Conservation Commission tends three trails that showcase different aspects of the outdoors, from bird-watching to geological history to scenic overlooks. A free trail guide is available at the Chamber of Commerce, and a self-guided walking tour takes you past a dozen historically significant buildings.

I can't promise a Smithsonian-sized experience at the **Littleton Area Historical Society** (1 Cottage St., 603/444-6435), since it's open only on Wednesdays. Built in 1905, the old opera house/fire station was renovated in 2001. If you're motivated—seriously motivated—the local society members will show you a Victorian melodeon and artifacts from the local glove company, and they will share the story of the Kilburn Brothers, who kicked off the DVD of their day—the stereographic view card.

Shopping

You could travel all over the nation to verify it, but it might be simpler just to believe **Chutters** (43 Main St., 603/444-5787, www.chutters.com) when it claims to be one of three general stores in America that still sells penny candy from a jar. That's 1,000 pieces of candy for a fin. Double that if you've got a sawbuck. It also features New Hampshire–made products and boasts the world's longest candy counter—and it's mighty long.

Blue-Plate Specials

While many cities offer an endless chain

Why Do Them Leaves Look Funny?

If you don't mind battling motor homes for the road, arrive during fall foliage when "leaf peepers" descend on New England like locusts on Kansas corn. They're here to watch the leaves change from a uniform green to an autumnal palette of oranges, reds, and yellows. Why do leaves change color? They don't, Gomer.

Here's the skinny: About two weeks before they "turn," a cell layer forms at the base of each leaf that prevents moisture from entering. The chlorophyll, which makes the leaf green, isn't able to renew itself, so the leaf's true color can be seen. Depending on exposure to the sun, elevation, and the chemical makeup of the tree, different colors appear. Sugar maple leaves are primarily red and orange, white ash turns yellow and purple, and the pin cherry's purple-green leaves turn yellow. Most color changes start at higher elevations and work their way down the mountains and hills.

of chain restaurants, Littleton is pleased to promote home-cooked comfort foods. **Topic of the Town** (30 Main St., 603/444-6721) offers another all-day breakfast, along with daily specials and turkey dinners, jumbo sirloin, Greek salads, chicken, ribs, and lovely frappes—all served in a generic diner setting. Perfect.

Drop by the **Littleton Diner** (145 Main St., 603/444-3994, www.littletondiner. com) for New England–style home-cooked food and a tasty reminder that not every restaurant needs million-dollar ad campaigns. Here since 1930, the diner serves breakfast anytime (try the pancakes), a roast turkey dinner, soups, salads, and sundaes, all amidst the satisfying clatter of diner flatware. The place is open daily for breakfast, lunch, and dinner, a testament to its tagline: There's Always Something Cooking.

Watering Holes

You'll find scant options for nightlife in Littleton, but, as a local observed, "This is New England, and that's how people like it." There's a tavern adjoining the **Italian Oasis Restaurant** (106 Main St., 603/444-6995) inside Parker Marketplace. The Oasis also has a microbrewery and serves mixed drinks.

Since there's not much shaking after dark, if a good flick is playing at **Jax Jr. Cinemas** (32 Main St., 603/444-5907), you'll want to stop in and relive the days when you hung out at the Saturday matinee. Quirky fact: This theater's claim to fame is that it premiered the 1930s Bette Davis movie *The Great Lie*. Locals are still abuzz.

Shut-Eye

There are campgrounds, cabins, and cottages listed on the chamber website. For more options on motels and campgrounds, call the Chamber of Commerce (603/444-6561, www.littletonareachamber.com).

Motels and Motor Courts

No unwanted surprises at **Eastgate Motor Inn** (335 Cottage St., Exit 41 at I-93, 603/444-3971, www.eastgatemotorinn.com).

This family-owned operation offers nicer-than-average rooms (some with a fridge) and above-average service, and it is usually booked by tourists who like a clean room, pool, free breakfast, and cash in their pocket. If you'd rather save your money for the road, consider this standard motel, with rates from around $74.

Inn-dependence

Thayer's Inn (136 Main St., 603/444-6469 or 800/634-8179, www.thayersinn. com) would seem perfectly at home in Mayberry. It opened in 1843 as a stage-coach stop, and some traditions continue. A few rooms still have shared baths, but all are clean and comfortable, with rates from around $70. This is a great place to stay if you're on a budget and even if you're not. President Grant gave a speech from the front balcony, but ask for a room in back—a lot of traffic rolls down Route 302. A continental breakfast is included in the rate.

Chain Drive

These chain hotels are in town, or within 10 miles of the city center:
Best Western
For more information, including phone numbers and websites, see page 99.

ON THE ROAD: LITTLETON TO CAMDEN

Get ready for a most excellent ride. This run offers three options: You can either take Route 302 across the White Mountains; you can drop south to reach Highway 112 (the famed Kancamagus); or make a day trip of both roads before doubling back the following day to reach Maine. If you can take only one road, take Highway 112.

The ride starts slowly. As you roll out of Littleton on Route 302 east, you'll pass the old Kilburn Brothers Stereoscopic View Factory. It's an apartment building now, but if you have any of these cards in your attic, now you'll know where they came from.

I once vowed to ride interstates only to pick up time (or, patriotic as I am, to serve the national interest). I make an exception for I-93 because this stretch rivals any back road you'll find. Follow it south toward the town of Lincoln where a detour at Exit 38 leads to the **Frost Place** (Ridge Rd., Franconia, 603/823-5510, www.frostplace. org, $5 donation), once the home of poet Robert Frost, who read his poem "The Gift Outright" at JFK's inauguration. Frost Place displays first editions of his books, photos, memorabilia, and a poet-in-residence who hosts readings in the old barn. Credit the harsh New Hampshire winters for a summers-only schedule: Memorial Day through Columbus Day.

Back on I-93, subtle hints such as towering mountains, plummeting roads, and a reduction to two lanes tell you you're entering Franconia Notch and dazzling eight-mile-long **Franconia Notch State Park** (603/823-8800, www.nhstateparks. com). Stuffed between the highest peaks of the Franconia and Kinsman ranges, this section of earth offers abundant places to explore. Pull off at the first exit (34C), and choose from swimming, camping, fishing, picnicking, and hiking around Echo Lake. Back on I-93, you'll jump on and off the road as you work your way south, taking the next exit (34B) to see the **New England Ski Museum** (603/823-7177, www. skimuseum.org, free). The base for the aerial tram here doubles as an information center for details on camping, hiking, and access to Profile Lake, and passage to the 4,200-foot peak of Cannon Mountain.

The next exit (34A) is near an 800-foot gorge called **The Flume** (www.visitnh.

gov/flume). If you can, make time for roughing it. Franconia Notch is a stunning park, and it's worth the layover to breathe fresh air and experience nature. There are no hotels in the park, but **Lafayette Campground** (603/823-9513, www.reserveamerica.com), with 97 tent sites, showers, and a store, places you at "Notch Central." Prior to May 3, 2003, this is where you could have looked up to see the "Old Man of the Mountain" (Nathaniel Hawthorne's Great Stone Face). Popularized in 1805, the natural granite profile disintegrated overnight in the fog and darkness and left a void for locals. Still, this section delivers The Basin that, like Keith Richards, is a 25,000-year-old glacial pothole.

Afterward, the going gets tricky, but stay on I-93 and watch for Exit 33 to get you onto Route 3 and into North Woodstock for a flirt with the past at **Clark's Trading Post** (603/745-8913, www.clarkstradingpost.com). It may seem corny, but this is a throwback to the days when you took road trips with your folks. Clark's has been at it for more than 75 years with trained bears, steam trains, and old-fashioned gadgets that tourists (circa 1962) love. Admission is $17. After Clark's, turn left onto a well-named connector road called "Connector Road," and at the next T, turn left to access Highway 112, the western tip of the Kancamagus Highway (known as "the Kanc").

Since the Kanc has no gas stations, stores, or hamburger clowns on its 34-mile stretch to Conway, the town of Lincoln has thoughtfully added a dense concentration of the type of urban congestion you're trying to escape. Race past these and soon you'll be in the midst of mind-boggling alpine scenery and rideable roads. Goose it and get into the rhythm of the road, but be prepared to brake when you reach some 20 mph hairpin turns and scenic viewing areas such as the Hancock Overlook.

Soon you'll learn that the road switches more frequently than Little Richard. You may head east, northwest, southeast, and then northeast to go east again. With the Kanc's multiple turns and seven-degree grades, you'll be hugging the centerline and shifting like a maniac.

After you cross Kancamagus Pass at 2,855 feet, you'll swoop down the mountain like a falcon, snatching great views to your left and following the road that now skirts the Swift River. To backtrack to Littleton and enjoy another winding and wild ride through forests and scenic overlooks, watch for Bear Notch Road that intersects the loop created by Highway 112 and Route 302, tosses in a tangle of roads, and at Route 302 can boomerang you back west.

Continuing east on the Kanc, you'll pass the **Rocky Gorge Scenic Area,** which leads to a wooden footbridge. Just over a mile later, you'll be at the Lower Falls, a great spot for a dip in the Swift River. Picnic spots, campgrounds, and riverfront rest areas mark the eastern edge of the highway, and with little fanfare, you'll reach the end of the road at Highway 113. The majority of traffic heads north to reach the outlet town of North Conway—but there's urban ugliness in this direction, my friend. Instead, start heading for the Maine coast via Route 302.

As state lines go, the entrance to Maine is minimalist—just a stark sign reading "Maine." My image of the state had been a frozen tundra where housewives carve blubber from dead seals. However, at first glance, you could put this road in Vermont or the Adirondacks. In earlier rides I headed towards the coast believing that I'd find wonderful oceanfront roads, but that turned out not to be so. That said, there's a nest of two-lane roads that reach into the preserved Maine wilderness. This is one of the best regions to do what motorcyclists love to do, and that's just to guide your ride across the state slowly towards the coast, grabbing any inland road that tempts you. If you're not ready to go off-script, get out your calculator since there are a number of numbers to follow over the next 135 miles.

A few miles over the border is Fryeburg where CR 5 takes you up towards Lovell. This is where you can split to the right on CR 93 east (aka Sweden Road) for about 10 miles before the road T's and you head north at CR 37 in South Waterford. The name is apt since there is water here—Bear Pond, Keoka Lake, McWain Pond—that you skirt around before CR 37 wraps up in East Waterford and CR 118. Take CR 118 east for about 15 miles towards the small towns of Norway and South Paris and by the time you roll into Norway, you'll be on CR 117, which is the only number you'll need to remember for about 25 miles. Now you have time to just skim down this slow and easy remote road all the way to the town of Leeds on the shores of Androscoggin Lake. It's a large lake, but not large enough to warrant a ferry here, so you have the undeniable pleasure to ride around its shores; first by taking CR 106 three miles up its west shore to the town of North Leeds, then completing the arc via county roads 219 and then 133 towards Winthrop and, finally, taking U.S. 202 east to Augusta.

While I try to avoid larger towns, I didn't mind going through Augusta because I knew it would take me to my ultimate goal, and that was getting onto CR 17. Its alias, Rockland Road, reveals that this path will take you on a slow descent all the way down to the coast—and it does it in style.

I was traveling in September, about a month before the peak of fall foliage, but already the beauty of nature was supernatural. For mile after mile there were ponds and small lakes and gentle rises and peaceful falls. There were nice fields and easy curves and a weirdly pristine natural landscape that looked as if a grounds crew had been tending to it for months. After listening to folks from Maine brag about their state, this seemed to reflect the essence of their pride. By the time I reached CR 90 at West Rockport, I realized I could have brought the ride to a quicker conclusion by jogging east to reach Rockport and Camden. Instead, I was into the ride so I continued south on 17 into Rockland which is accented by a beautiful harbor and decked out with an old-fashioned active downtown. Rockland includes some great diners and plenty of evidence that the town takes pride in presenting the **Maine Lobster Festival** (207/596-0376 or 800/562-2529, www.mainelobsterfestival.com) each August.

If there's time, hang around Rockland. When it's time to head out, it's only a few miles via U.S. 1 north to reach beautiful Camden. Of course, if you're still ready to roll, you can just turn south on U.S. 1 and about 1,900 miles later, you'll reach the end of the road in Key West, Florida.

I think Camden makes more sense.

ALTERNATE ROUTE: ROUTE 302

Although the Kancamagus Highway is an obvious choice, following Route 302 out of Littleton is a close second. After passing through the center of town, turn left at the Eastgate Motor Inn. It's an inauspicious beginning, but soon the road turns mighty pretty.

Route 302 leads to Fosters Crossroads, where you'll start a southeast descent toward Bretton Woods and the famous **Mount Washington Inn** (603/278-1000 or 800/314-1752, www.mountwashingtonresort.com), which sits majestically off to your left. If you can't spot the white frame palace and its red roof, follow the sightline of tourists who have it pinned down with cameras and binoculars. Staying at the grand hotel can be an expensive option, but looking is free. The inn boasts fantastic views of the White Mountains bordered by the Presidential Range, as well as all the amenities that make this a resort: horseback riding, tennis, entertainment, and an 18-hole Donald Ross course. Add to this the 900-foot white-railed veranda and broad porte-cochère, and you know you're riding into the lap of luxury. If the inn is full, it books the Bretton Woods Motor Inn and Townhomes at Bretton Woods as well.

On your left in Bretton Woods, you'll see the ingenious **Mount Washington Cog Railway** (603/278-5404 or 800/922-8825, www.thecog.com), which takes passengers to the chilly peak of Mount Washington. At 6,288 feet, Mount Washington is the highest point in the Northeast—called Agiocochook by Native Americans and believed to be the home of the Great Spirit. Settlers Abel Crawford and his son Ethan carved out the first footpath to its summit in 1819. That footpath is still in use. If you're fascinated by all things mechanical, you'll be impressed by how this railroad can ascend a 37-degree grade. The three-hour tour isn't cheap—$59 for adults. Then again, this *is* the highest peak in New England… then again, it is $59. Then again, the train *is* called Old Peppersass….

Farther on, you'll ride past Saco Lake and enter dazzling Crawford Notch, as the road slices into the folds of the mountains and begins to loosely follow the Saco River toward Bartlett. For the next six miles, you'll encounter the unspoiled rugged beauty of the Presidential Range. **Crawford Notch State Park** (603/374-2272, www.nhstateparks.org) offers picnic areas, hiking, waterfalls, and a visitors center. After an exhilarating run through the notch, you'll reach Glen and the junction of Route 16, which leads north to the **Mount Washington Auto Road** (603/466-3988, www.mountwashingtonautoroad.com). Although it's several miles north in Gorham, riding up Mount Washington is worth the detour if it's worth $14 to tackle eight miles of 12-degree grades and wind speeds clocked at 231 mph (back in 1934). If so, put your visor down and chain yourself to your seat. Open only from mid-May to late October, the road provides killer views of the White Mountains, Presidential Range, and beyond. If you haven't been blown off the mountain, double back to Route 302 and head for the coast.

CAMDEN PRIMER

Tourism bureaus tend to go overboard promoting their town or state. Camden is different. It actually delivers on its promise of beauty. This harbor town is where the mountains (Appalachians) meet the sea (Atlantic), and the confluence makes a dramatic setting.

Although Camden is approximately the same size as Littleton, the village is far more active. Robert Ripley once estimated that if all Chinese citizens marched four abreast, they could walk around the world and the march would never end. That's about true for traffic here during Camden's peak season. Of course, that's on a nice day with warm weather. Fog and gray rains wash in and out frequently and can turn a great ride into a desolate and depressingly wet mess.

Laconia Motorcycle Week

A year after 400 riders spent a few days at Weirs Beach, New Hampshire, the first sanctioned "Gypsy Tour" was held in Laconia in 1917. Popular with America's few thousand riders, the Gypsy Tour developed a following through the 1920s and 1930s. In 1938, motorcycle hill-climber Fritzie Baer and his partners (the Red Hat Brigade) started a 30-year effort to keep the rally at full steam. But during the 1960s, the hill climbs and road races were cancelled as the rally fell out of favor with local police.

Things came to a head a week before the 1965 rally when a state law was passed giving police authority to arrest riders who loitered in groups of three or more. That was bound to spark trouble, and it did. At the "Riot of Laconia," motorcyclists battled police and the National Guard which helped diminish Motorcycle Week into Motorcycle Weekend. In 1975, camping along Highway 106 was outlawed and the rally continued to lose steam and attendance dropped to a new low of 25,000. But as the Sturgis and Daytona rallies grew in size and popularity, locals took a fresh look at Laconia. In 1991, Motorcycle Week was back, the term "Gypsy Tour" came back the following year, and the hill climbs returned to Gunstock the year after that.

Today, hundreds of thousands of motorcyclists arrive for nine days of motorcycle events, including races, hill climbs, touring, parades, vintage bikes, swap meets, demo rides, and the blessing of the motorcycles. The rally (603/366-2000, www.laconiamcweek.com) is held annually in mid-June.

As in most New England towns worth visiting, the central district is best seen on foot. Adjacent to the marina, you'll find a large parking lot with motorcycle-reserved spaces. From there, you can set off to eat seafood, browse bookshops, check out local crafts, eat seafood, cruise on a schooner, and eat seafood.

Summertime, obviously, is peak tourist season, with a very affluent group setting up shop and tourists arriving for the windjammer cruises that set sail from the harbor. Big, fat money rolls in from banking families, cruise line owners, and personalities like John Travolta, Kirstie Alley, and Martha Stewart, who arrive to buy large properties and even entire islands. But after they've left and the tourists are gone, the locals get back to work.

So here it is. It's not a wild town, but if you appreciate nature, you won't find a better base for day trips to search out Maine's best roads and natural attractions.

ON THE ROAD: CAMDEN

To see the best of Camden, you'll need at least two very full days. Reserve part of the first sunny day for a ride to Mount Battie. Leaving town on U.S. 1 North, you'll enjoy nice elevation changes for about two miles before reaching **Camden Hills State Park** (207/236-3109). Fork over $4.50, and you can ascend the 1.6-mile road in a steady, steep climb and reach the 790-foot summit of Mount Battie a few minutes later. Although the ride is short, you'll remember the view for a thousand years. From a stone tower lookout, you'll see the ocean meeting the mountains a few miles distant. The effect is spiritual. The sun shines so brightly on the water that the ocean looks like an endless white desert. Small islands break off from the mainland; roofs sprout through the tops of fir trees; small coves shelter schooners; and the wakes of clipper ships look like wisps of cotton. On a clear day, as your eyes follow the coast northeast to Bar Harbor's Cadillac Mountain (more than 40 miles away), it seems as if you can see forever.

PULL IT OVER: CAMDEN HIGHLIGHTS
Attractions and Adventures

In Camden satisfaction comes from seeing the world by your bike and someone else's boat. A fleet of schooners takes two-hour cruises around Penobscot Bay that put you among coastal mountains, seals, eagles, porpoises, and lobster boats. As you check out different charters, ask if you'll be able to help raise the sails, take the wheel, or simply kick back with a beer or wine. Costs are usually about $30. Options include the 65-foot windjammer *Appledore* (Camden Town Landing, Sharp's Wharf, 207/236-8353, www.appledore2.com) and schooner *Lazy Jack II* (Camden Town Landing, 207/230-0602, www.schooner-lazyjack.com), a 13-passenger 1947 Bahamian charter boat restored and brought to Camden in 1987. The schooner *Surprise* (Camden Town Landing, 207/236-4687, www.camdenmainesailing.com) is a 44-foot, 1918 classic on which Captain Jack serves cookies and fruit and spins yarns. Schooner *Olad* (Camden Town Landing, Sharp's Wharf, 207/236-2323, www.maineschooners.com) offers a 57-foot windjammer that departs every hour with 21–40 passengers.

Want to stay at sea overnight or longer?

Check out the deluxe **Maine Windjammer Cruises** (Camden Town Landing, 207/236-2938 or 800/736-7981, www.mainewindjammercruises.com) for weekend, four-day, and week-long cruises departing Monday and Friday. Promoted as America's oldest windjammer, the *Lewis R. French* (Camden Town Landing, 800/469-4635, www.schoonerfrench.com) offers three- to six-day cruises for up to 22 nonsmoking crewmembers.

For fishing trips, contact **Georges River Outfitters** (1384 Atlantic Hwy., Warren, 207/273-3818, www.sportsmensgifts.com). Native Maineiac Jeff Bellmore is a United States Coast Guard captain and master Maine guide who hosts customized fresh- and saltwater excursions and limits boats to two passengers for one-on-one (or -two) advice. Freshwater catches include salmon, bass, trout, and perch; ocean runs are for stripers, bluefish, and mackerel. If you've got a few hundred bucks, then Georges River Outfitters has a captain, boat, and guide for you.

Maine's great outdoors has inspired generations of artists. Several miles east of Camden, **The Farnsworth Art Museum** (16 Museum St., Rockland, 207/596-6457, www.farnsworthmuseum.org) displays one of the larger collections of works by the Wyeths of Maine, recognized as the first family of American art. Additional works reflect all eras, from colonial to American impressionism to the present, with 8,000 items on display. Admission is $12.

You may want to make tracks to see the collection at the impressive **Owls Head Transportation Museum** (Rte. 73, Owls Head, 207/594-4418, www.ohtm.org). Located a few miles south and west of Camden, the mechanical menagerie here includes a 1937 Mercedes 540K, a World War I Fokker tri-plane, a Stanley Steamer, a 1963 prototype Mustang, a 1938 Indian Junior Scout, and a crazy contraption called the Scripps—Booth Bi-Autogo (a two-wheeled automobile/motorcycle that features Detroit's first V-8 engine). The displays are dazzling—and fun. Summer events include an antique motorcycle show featuring more than 200 vintage bikes.

If you're inspired to further explore the wilderness, a few hours from Camden are two businesses that are worth a side trip. **Northern Outdoors** (207/663-4466 or 800/765-7238, www.northernoutdoors.com) and **New England Outdoor Center** (207/723-5438 or 800/766-7238, www.neoc.com) coordinate adventures for all things Maine. They can help arrange rafting, fishing, climbing, canoeing, kayaking, whitewater rafting, hunting, and fishing excursions.

Blue-Plate Specials

Cappy's (1 Main St., 207/236-2254, www.cappyschowder.com) is the place for bikers, sailors, locals, and anyone who likes good food and good service. You'll find real clam chowder, crab skins, and shrimp—and those are just the appetizers. Come here at night, and the lively bar talk will surely include conversation about boats, bikes, and microbrews such as Old Thumper, Goat Island Light, and Blue Fin Stout. Microbrew tastings are held in Cappy's crow's nest from 4 to 6 p.m.

Besides Mount Battie, the best view in town is of the harbor. Sit on the deck at the **Waterfront Restaurant** (40 Bayview St., 207/236-3747, www.waterfrontcamden.com), and the harbor is yours—along with lobster, steak, and an oyster bar. The full bar is open until the customers go home.

Watering Holes

You'd think that a seaport town would have a host of pubs where sailors could drink and compare parrots, but most grog is served in civilized restaurants here. If you're looking for a place to drink, in addition to Cappy's bar, you can head down the alley and hang out at **Gilbert's Public House** (Bayview Landing, 207/236-4320) for cold brews and live bands.

Shut-Eye
Motels and Motor Courts
Camden still has some old-fashioned motels. Consider the **Towne Motel** (68 Elm St., 207/236-3377 or 800/656-4999, www.camdenmotel.com). In the heart of town (and the closest motel to the harbor), it has 18 rooms that start at $109 in peak season and drop considerably in shoulder seasons. A light continental breakfast is included. North of town is the classic **Birchwood Motel** (Belfast Rd., 207/236-4204, www.birchwoodmotel.com), where summer rates for the 15 oceanview rooms range between $89 and $109. You'll love its clean, old-school look.

Inn-dependence
The Belmont Inn (6 Belmont Ave., 207/236-8053 or 800/238-8053, www.thebelmontinn.com) is two blocks off U.S. 1 and offers 10 times the solitude you might expect. Wraparound porches, a great sitting room, breakfasts on the porch, and 99 windows give this private house a serious breath of fresh, outdoor air. The large rooms have a distinctly homey feel, and high season rates start at around $200. If the day's ride has worn you out and you can afford the privilege, this is quite a nice option.

Chain Drive
These chain hotels are in town, or within 10 miles of the city center:
Best Western, Hampton Inn
For more information, including phone numbers and websites, see page 99.

CAMDEN TO BAR HARBOR

After hanging around Camden long enough to get your soul recharged, it's time to hit the road, Jack. The sad fact is that even though you're heading up one of the most striking coastlines in America, you won't see much of it unless you're offshore on a lobster boat. If you sift through the rubble, the mundane views reveal a few jewels, such as the bridge at Verona, but mostly you'll see traffic clogging the main artery to Mount Desert Island, part of Acadia National Park. Stick with U.S. 1 until Ellsworth, where you can take Route 3 south into what the locals call "Bah Haabah."

At Hulls Cove, look for the **Visitors Center** (207/288-3338, www.nps.gov/acad). Rangers at the center offer volumes of material, from the *Beaver Log* newspaper to information on ranger-led programs, weather, tides, fishing, and camping. A free film narrated by Jack Perkins (of *A&E Biography* fame) tells the story of how "Rusticators" from elite circles in Philadelphia, Boston, and New York popularized the island. Money from the likes of Pulitzer, Ford, Vanderbilt, and J. P. Morgan financed mansions patronizingly called "cottages."

For motorcycle travelers, the most relevant information pertains to the 27-mile Park Loop Road, which follows the island's coast and then knifes its way through the center of the park. You could race it in an hour, but allow three for abundant photo ops. If you have a sound system, spring for an Acadia audio tour; if not, a cheaper paperback booklet should suffice. Either will fill you in on the island's history and natural beauty. A few highlights:

It was John D. Rockefeller who advanced the design of 45 miles of carriage roads, created with the stipulation that no motor cars would be allowed (he never mentioned motorcycles). In any event, this was a summer haven for rich folks and they all felt so privileged to have this hideaway that, in 1919, they agreed to donate well over 30,000 acres of mountains, lakes, and sea to the government. Not only was it an incredibly nice gesture, it made Acadia the first national park east of the Mississippi. Everything was going swell until 1947

At Home in Maine

Maine's residents are called "Mainers" or "Maineiacs." If you're not from here, friend, you're "from away."

Like the rest of America, Maine is threatened by the "national village." The Maine accent ("Ayuh, the clomms ah hahmless") is in danger of turning into a Midwestern drone as kids pick up vanilla speech patterns from the tube. The other assault comes from rich outsiders, who made their stash and now want to buy a piece of charming Maine. After they arrive, instead of appreciating the state for what it is, they try to re-create what they left behind, sometimes posting "No Trespassing" signs on beaches where natives had walked for years. According to one Maineiac, "It pisses us off." The bright side, he adds, is that folks "from away" usually last only four or five years before leaving "'coz they can't take the weather, anyway."

Ayuh.

when what became known as the Great Forest Fire swept over most of the island and burned more than 17,000 acres to cinders. Also lost in the conflagration were the mansions of "Millionaire's Row." Good heavens, Lovey...charcoal!

In peak season, a $20 fee ($10 during the shoulder seasons) grants you access to the Park Loop Road, and you'll immediately appreciate the efforts of the people who gave us the gift of Acadia. In addition to the main road, branches lead off to less trafficked sections of the park, although nearly every road leads to great cliff corners, dips, and rises. Scenic ocean views are frequent, and if you time it right you'll arrive when the normally silent Thunder Hole booms with the full fury of the sea. If there's fog, the landscape becomes an impressionist painting. If you're riding on a clear day, the peak of Cadillac Mountain (1,532 feet) may afford a matching view of Camden's Mount Battie—and exposure to the first rays of sunlight to fall on the United States.

When you've looped the park and had your fill of beauty, you can roll into downtown Bar Harbor where tourist central is comprised of a village green and mismatched buildings that house bookstores, drugstores, and the ever-present gift shops. Considering you've ridden this far, it's all worth checking out.

PULL IT OVER: BAR HARBOR HIGHLIGHTS
Attractions and Adventures

Like Camden, Bar Harbor's season runs from about mid-May to late October—weather willing. The best attractions here are the outdoor activities, which is why deep-sea fishing charters, windjammer cruises, island cruises, lighthouse cruises, and kayak rentals abound. The town pier is the best place to pick up brochures and make your selection.

Want to get out of the saddle and up a mountain? You can learn the ropes at **Atlantic Climbing School** (26 Cottage St., 207/288-2521, www.climbacadia.com), with beginner to advanced programs that take you to Acadia for instruction on spectacular cliffs bordered by the sea. Prices run $70–250, depending on the sort of climbing you'll be doing and the number of people in the class. If you've got time, get a piece of the rock. Reservations are required.

If you prefer getting away from the crowds and captains, charter a boat. Ask what's included—fuel can be expensive. **Mansell Boat Rentals** (135 Shore Rd., Manset, 207/244-5625, www.mansellboatrentals.com) rents a variety of boats, from sailboats to Boston Whalers. Experience is necessary, a deposit is required, and you'll have access to some of the finest sea and shores in the nation.

Coastal Kayaking Tours (48 Cottage St., 207/288-9605 or 800/526-8615, www.acadiafun.com), Maine's oldest sea kayak outfitter, has more than 100 sea kayaks, 20 trainers, guides, and tours that can last from a few hours to a few days. You'll get a hearty upper-body workout and the opportunity to watch sea life from sea level.

Having done a similar tour on Cape Cod, I can vouch for the amazing sights that appear on a whale-watching charter. Offered from late May to late October, **Bar Harbor Whale Watch Co.** (207/288-2386 or 888/942-5474, www.whalesrus.com) will take you out on trips that last around three hours. You'd think that spotting a whale would be a rarity, but generally the pilot can track them down from the telltale spout and then maneuver the boat so close that you can actually see the huge humpback, finback, and minke whales drifting just below the surface. Be sure to wear your leathers, since it can get cold on the boat. They also offer lobster fishing, seal watching, and sunset cruises.

It sounds kind of odd, but you may appreciate the collection at the **Wendell Gilley Museum of Bird Carving** (corner of Main and Herrick Sts., Southwest Harbor, 207/244-7555, www.wendellgilleymuseum.org). It's slightly out of the way in Southwest Harbor, but worth it if you need a fantastically detailed bird carving for your office. Gilley, a late native son, earned a national following, and you'll see why when you examine the intricately carved songbirds, shorebirds, eagles, and other birds of prey. Incredible. The museum shop sells bird carvings, carving tools, and field guides for nature lovers. Hours vary, so call ahead.

Shopping

If you're a devotee of America's million-plus microbreweries, you'll be happy to find the **Atlantic Brewing Company** (15 Knox Rd., 207/288-2337, www.atlanticbrewing.com) in rural Bar Harbor. Stock up on Bar Harbor Real Ale, a nut brown ale with a round, malty body. Other brews include Blueberry Ale, Ginger Wheat, and the cleverly named Coal Porter. Choice two is the **Bar Harbor Brewing Company** (8 Mount Desert St., 207/288-4592, www.barharborbrewing.com), which has received first-place finishes in world beer championships with brews like Thunder Hole Ale and Cadillac Mountain Stout. Both offer free tours.

After a hard ride, it's time for the great indoors and a good cigar. In the summertime, **Joe's Smoke Shop** (119 Main St., 207/288-2886) has enough cigars to fill a walk-in humidor. Plus, there's an intimate bar where you can enjoy a martini or a glass of wine, brandy, port, or scotch.

Blue-Plate Specials

How many diners can back up a "Get in Here and Eat!" sign with great food? Since 1969, **Bar Harbor Route 66 Restaurant** (21 Cottage St., 207/288-3708, www.bhroute66.com), a funky, collectibles-filled diner, has served roadhouse specialties like chicken pot pies and hot turkey dinners, as well as fish and pasta. It's open for lunch and dinner, with happy hour from 5 until "66 minutes past" (6:06 P.M.).

The Thirsty Whale Tavern (40 Cottage St., 207/288-9335, www.thistywhaletavern.com) offers fine spirits, sandwiches, and beer in a basic bar—uh, tavern—setting. You'll find chicken, burgers, haddock, clams, and a dozen beers, including some microbrews, on tap.

Galyn's Galley Restaurant (17 Main St., 207/288-9706, www.galynsbarharbor.com) was constructed inside an 1890s boarding house, so you can check in and check out fresh lobster, scallops, fish, and the specialty prime rib. Upstairs, the intimate lounge features an antique mahogany bar. If you don't drink alcohol, just order one of the homemade, super sweet desserts, chased with a shot of insulin.

Shut-Eye

If you have to stay over, Bar Harbor has more than 3,000 hotel rooms. Check www.barharborinfo.com for listings. If the weather's right, camping is another option. Campsites within Acadia National Park need to be reserved well in advance. Call the National Parks Reservations service at 800/365-2267, or go to www.recreation.gov.

Chain Drive

These chain hotels are in town, or within 10 miles of the city center:
Best Western, Days Inn, Fairfield Inn, Holiday Inn, Quality Inn
For more information, including phone numbers and websites, see page 99.

Resources for Riders

White Mountains–Blue Seas Run

Maine Travel Information
Maine Campground Owners Association—207/782-5874, www.campmaine.com
Maine Office of Tourism—888/624-6345, www.visitmaine.com
Maine Road Conditions—866/282-7578, www.511maine.gov

New Hampshire Travel Information
New Hampshire Fish and Game Department—603/271-3421,
   www.wildlife.state.nh.us
New Hampshire Office of Travel and Tourism—603/271-2343 or
   800/386-4664, www.visitnh.gov
New Hampshire Road Conditions—866/282-7579, www.511nh.com
New Hampshire State Parks—603/271-3556, www.nhparks.state.nh.us

Local and Regional Information
Acadia National Park Information—207/288-3338, www.nps.gov/acad
Bar Harbor Chamber of Commerce—207/288-5103 or 800/288-5103,
   www.barharborinfo.com
Camden Chamber of Commerce—207/236-4404 or 800/223-5459,
   www.camdenme.org
Littleton Chamber of Commerce—603/444-6561,
   www.littletonareachamber.com or www.golittleton.com
Mount Washington Valley Chamber of Commerce—603/356-5701 or
   800/367-3364, www.mtwashingtonvalley.org
White Mountain National Forest—603/528-8721, www.fs.fed.us/r9/white

Maine Motorcycle Shops
Big Moose Harley-Davidson/Buell—375 Riverside St., Portland, 207/797-6061
   or 800/427-5393, www.bigmooseharley.com
North Country Harley-Davidson—3099 N. Belfast Ave., Augusta, 207/622-7994
   or 800/934-1653, www.northcountryhd.com
Reid's Cycle—1300 Atlantic Hwy., Northport, 207/338-6068,
   www.reidscycle.com

New Hampshire Motorcycle Shops
Laconia Harley-Davidson—239 Daniel Webster Hwy. (Rte. 3), Meredith,
   603/279-4526, www.laconiaharley.com
Littleton Harley-Davidson/Buell—Rte. 116, Bethlehem, 603/444-1300,
   www.littletonharley.com
Littleton Motorsports—515 Union St., Littleton, 603/444-5003,
   www.littletonmotorsports.com
Manchester Harley-Davidson/Buell—115 John E. Devine Dr., Manchester,
   603/622-2461 or 800/292-5393, www.manchesterhd.com
White Mountain Harley-Davidson—1275 White Mountain Hwy., North
   Conway, 603/356-7775

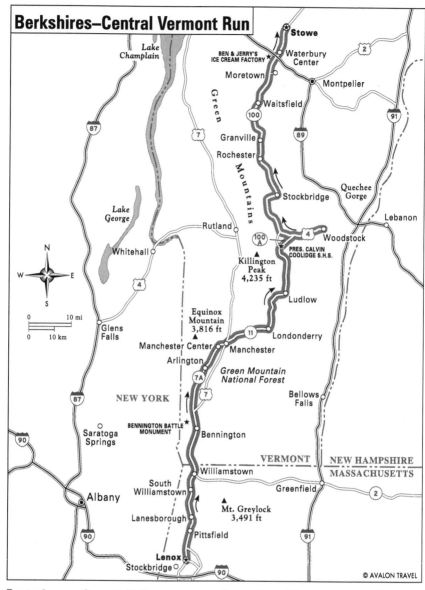

Berkshires–Central Vermont Run

Route: Lenox to Stowe via Williamstown, Arlington, Manchester Village, Plymouth Notch, Woodstock, Rochester, Waitsfield

Distance: Approximately 210 miles

First Leg: Lenox, Massachusetts to Woodstock, Vermont (122 miles)

Second Leg: Woodstock to Stowe, Vermont (88 miles)

Helmet Laws: Massachusetts and Vermont require helmets.

Berkshires–Central Vermont Run

Lenox, Massachusetts to Stowe, Vermont

If you live west of the Mississippi or south of the Mason-Dixon line, reaching your region's best roads can take hours. This is where New England is different. The dense concentration of rivers, hillocks, and mountains compresses a nation's worth of ideal motorcycling roads into a relatively small area. Of course, it's not just the roads that make this trip one of the best in America. This tour fulfills the criteria for a perfect run: culture, history, and scenery.

In Lenox, you'll find culture in abundance at novelist Edith Wharton's home, The Mount, in summer stock theaters, and at Tanglewood (the summer venue of the Boston Symphony Orchestra). A short ride away is Stockbridge, Norman Rockwell's final hometown. From the heart of the Berkshires, fantastic road leads to Vermont and historic Plymouth Notch, the preserved village and birthplace of the reticent yet surprisingly eloquent Calvin Coolidge. Neighboring Woodstock is the quintessential New England village and your final destination, Stowe, is as enjoyable in mild weather as it is when skiers arrive in winter.

LENOX PRIMER

In the latter half of the 1800s, this tranquil farming region was "discovered" by famous and wealthy residents of Boston and New York. First, Nathaniel Hawthorne wrote *The House of Seven Gables* and *Tanglewood Tales* while living near Lenox, and then Samuel Gray Ward, the Boston banker who later helped finance the purchase of Alaska, built a summer home near Hawthorne's cottage. Through Hawthorne's words and Ward's wealthy friends, Lenox became *the* place to establish summer homes that were, in fact, gigantic mansions their owners sloughed off as "cottages." In Lenox, actors, authors, bankers, and industrialists like Andrew Carnegie added flash to the Gilded Age.

Around the turn of the 20th century, a federal income tax overturned the fortunes of many of these families, and the mansions were later sold with many being converted into the schools, hotels, and resorts you'll see today. Although it lost a few millionaires, Lenox found new life through music. In 1937, locals enlisted the Boston Symphony Orchestra to make Tanglewood—an estate between Lenox and Stockbridge—its summer home. Today, Tanglewood hosts one of the world's leading music festivals and has made this town the summertime cultural capital of the Northeast.

If you travel here in the peak season of July and August, be warned that prices—especially for dining and lodging—rise dramatically. Then again, the upscale attitude hasn't sidelined local favorites like breakfast diners and working-class bars.

Take it all in, then in the evening when the streets are quiet and the moon is rising over the Berkshire hills, walk through the Lenox streets. The evening mist, historic buildings, and peaceful silence will transport you back 200 years.

ON THE ROAD: LENOX

The core of Lenox is small. Small, I tell ya, just two blocks wide and about four blocks long. You could goose it and clear town in less than ten seconds. But that's not what Lenox is about. And since parking is free, rest your bike. The longer you stay, the more you save.

Take your time and see the primary street (Church Street); walk along Main Street (Route 7A); and drop down back alleys to discover less trafficked antique shops, art galleries, and coffee bars. Stop by the circa 1815 Berkshire County Courthouse, which now houses the Lenox Library.

Since Lenox proper doesn't offer a wealth of roads, think about investing a half day on an extremely casual and educational short loop to neighboring Stockbridge. Even during peak tourist season,

the back roads are lightly traveled and immensely fun.

In the heart of town, the Paterson memorial obelisk marks the intersection of Route 7A and Route 183 South. Head down Route 183 and you've entered a canopy road that runs past a lake called the Stockbridge Bowl, which you can reach by turning left down Hawthorne Street. When you reach it, you'll discover that this glacial lake is reserved for the residents of Stockbridge (if you're discreet I doubt you'll get carded). This is a perfect place to swim, blessed with an amazing vista of the surrounding Berkshires.

Back on Route 183, Tanglewood will soon appear on your left. Since concerts don't begin until dusk, keep riding straight for several more tree-lined miles until you cross Route 102 to reach the Norman Rockwell Museum on your left. Farther down Route 183 on your right is Chesterwood, the equally fascinating home and studio of sculptor Daniel Chester French—best known for his masterpiece, the Lincoln sculpture within the Lincoln Memorial. His studio is still cluttered with several Lincoln studies and other striking pieces.

Return to Route 102 East, and you'll enter the village of Stockbridge, where you can stop for a drink at the Lion's Den inside the famous **Red Lion Inn** (Main St., corner of Rtes. 7 and 102, 413/298-5545, www.redlioninn.com), which has been serving travelers since 1773. Naturally, there are a few gift shops and restaurants in town—although none of special note. When you're ready to ride back to Lenox, return to Route 7 North (turn left at the fire station) and watch for Berkshire Cottages Blantyre and Cranwell on your right, quite visible examples of the magnitude of the wealth that once resided in these hills.

Just ahead, Route 7A splits off to the

left. Follow that and soon you'll find you've completed a soothing circle tour. Now you're back home in Lenox.

PULL IT OVER: LENOX HIGHLIGHTS
Attractions and Adventures

During July and August, the Boston Symphony Orchestra gets the hell out of Beantown and heads to **Tanglewood** (West St./Rte. 183, 413/637-5165 or 617/637-5165, www.bso.org). The site of the world's leading music festival, Tanglewood has been drawing crowds since 1937 and is a must-see if you're here in season. Guest conductors, including Andre Prévin and John Williams, have taken the lead beneath The Shed, and non-BSO summer nights feature such artists as YoYo Ma, Garrison Keillor, and James Taylor. Before you go, pack a blanket and swing by **Loeb's Food Town** (42 Main St., 413/637-0270), a great little downtown grocery where you can pick up a baked chicken, beer, wine, and everything else for your evening under the stars. Lawn tickets are reasonably priced, which makes this perhaps the best outdoor concert venue in America—and the best musical picnic you'll ever enjoy.

Edith Wharton, one of America's most celebrated authors, foreshadowed this book's success by winning the 1921 Pulitzer Prize for *The Age of Innocence.* You'd be surprised just how contemporary her works remain. Wharton's restored estate, **The Mount** (2 Plunkett St., Rtes. 7 and 7A, 413/551-5111, www.edithwharton.org, tours $16), was built in 1902 based on the classical precepts of her book *The Decoration of Houses.* Tours are conducted daily May through October and present a great way to experience the Berkshires as Wharton might have. A biography lecture series takes place on Mondays and readings from her books are presented on the verandah on Wednesdays.

Highbrow bikers look forward to **Shakespeare & Company** (70 Kemble St., 413/637-1197, www.shakespeare.org), which is near The Mount and stages plays by Shakespeare as well as Berkshire playwrights in three theaters year-round.

A quiet and natural destination to ride your bike, not to mention a peaceful place to get centered in the morning, **Berkshire Wildlife Sanctuaries** (472 W. Mountain Rd., 413/637-0320, $4) is just a few miles from town. In season the trails are open dawn–dusk daily. Part of the larger 1,500-acre Pleasant Valley Sanctuary, the Berkshire section offers several miles of walking trails and abundant wildlife.

Norman Rockwell was the Charles Kuralt of canvas, capturing an America that existed only in our minds. While the somewhat stark **Norman Rockwell Museum** (Rte. 183, Stockbridge, 413/298-4100, www.nrm.org, $15, add $5 for an audio tour) doesn't exactly capture his sincerity, it does display the world's largest collection of his original art, with nearly 500 works. The collection includes the original *Four Freedoms,* an inspiring series on American ideals that alone makes this museum well worth the ride. Outside the museum, you'll find Rockwell's former studio. It was moved here and now appears as it did when he worked on his pivotal work, *The Golden Rule.* Before you leave, one must-have souvenir is his autobiography which reveals that this seemingly easygoing man had a rambling life filled with a passion for excellence. Just right for reading on the road, you can pick up a copy here. The museum and store are open 10 A.M.–5 P.M. daily.

You may not know the name Daniel Chester French, but I guarantee that you know the work of this American sculptor.

A few blocks from the Rockwell Museum is **Chesterwood** (4 Williamsville Rd., Stockbridge, 413/298-3579, www.chesterwood.org, $10), a 122-acre Italian-style villa where he created masterpieces like the monumental Lincoln sculpture that's part of the Lincoln Memorial (1922) and Concord's Minute Man (1875). After viewing his home and seeing some 500-plus works in the well-stocked studio, stroll the grounds and you'll likely sense the power of the natural surroundings that inspired these works of Americana. Chesterwood is open 10 A.M.–5 P.M. daily.

Herman Melville lived in **Arrowhead** (780 Holmes Rd., Pittsfield, 413/442-1793, www.mobydick.org, $12) from 1850 to 1863, writing books such as *Moby-Dick*. After the world traveler and gifted writer found it difficult to raise a family on modest royalties, he packed it up for a desk job in New York City where he worked for the last 19 years of his life as a customs inspector. Arrowhead is loaded with many of Melville's personal artifacts, and if you like his books, then it's worth the detour. The home is open 9:30 A.M.–5 P.M. Memorial Day–Columbus Day, with tours on the hour.

Blue-Plate Specials

On my last visit to Lenox, I noticed that three of my affordable favorites—a pizza place, a breakfast joint, and a downhome café—had folded. For those sort of places, you'll have to travel down to Great Barrington or up towards Pittsfield. But there is a cost-conscious option in Lenox: **The Scoop** (26 Housatonic St., 413/637-9192, www.scooplenox.com) promotes its ice creams and sorbets, but they also serve diner-style breakfasts all day, and at lunch and dinner the menu showcases burgers, wraps, and classic sandwiches.

A few miles north of Lenox en route to Pittsfield on Route 7, the **Dakota** (1035 South St., 413/499-7900, www.steakseafood.com/dak), has been serving big food in a big Pacific Northwest setting since the 1960s. The featured items include fresh salmon, prime rib, lobster, and hand-cut steaks. Expect to wait for a table. Expect the meal to last for days.

Watering Holes

Want to look like a local? Pull up a barstool at the **Olde Heritage Tavern** (912 Housatonic St., 413/637-0884). It offers all the ingredients of a neighborhood bar: Foosball, darts, jukeboxes, local characters, pub grub (burgers, wings, pizzas, liquor, and pitchers of Newcastle Brown Ale and others). Not just a bar—this is a New England tavern. Last call is 12:30 A.M.

Shut-Eye

Lenox has dozens of inns and a healthy number of independent motels. In high season, many inns and hotels require minimum stays on weekends, and prices rise accordingly, so check in advance. Three lodging services can help you: For countywide reservations contact the **Berkshire Visitors Bureau** (888/256-7480 or 413/743-4500, www.berkshires.org); you can also check the **Chamber of Commerce**'s (www.lenox.org/lodging) listing of local digs; or, if you prefer to stay south of town in Lee, Lenoxdale, Stockbridge, or Great Barrington, the **Berkshire Lodging Association** (413/528-4006, www.berkshirelodging.com) offers a list of inns, hotels, and motels.

Inn-dependence

Even with 31 rooms and suites at three neighboring houses, the woods surrounding the **Cornell Inn** (203 Main St., 413/637-0562 or 800/637-0562, www.cornellinn.com, $80–110 high season) provide an intimate and comfortable setting. There's a pond and patio area to enjoy when the weather's right. The service is friendly and the homey room styles range from Colonial to Victorian.

Dig deep if you'd like to stay at **Garden Gables Inn** (135 Main St., 413/637-0193 or 888/243-0193, www.lenoxinn.com, $190 and up on weekends in high season). Although it's on the main drag, the setting is secluded and peaceful with five acres providing a buffer from the tourists. A swimming pool and comfortable rooms make this a safe and relaxing choice.

Chain Drive

These chain hotels are in town, or within 10 miles of the city center:

Best Western, Comfort Inn, Econo Lodge, Hampton Inn, Holiday Inn Howard Johnson, Knights Inn, Quality Inn, Ramada, Rodeway, Super 8, Travelodge

For more information, including phone numbers and websites, see page 99.

ON THE ROAD: LENOX TO WOODSTOCK

When you leave Lenox, Route 7A merges with Route 7 on the road to Pittsfield. While tense traffic is the price you'll pay to reach the Berkshire County seat, you'll be duly rewarded when you take a one-block detour to the nondescript **King Kone** (133 Fenn St., 413/496-9485), at the corner of Fenn and 1st Streets in Pittsfield. Just $1.70 buys either a small, medium, or large cone at this old-fashioned ice cream shack. Go for the large. It doesn't cost any more, it's nearly a foot tall and, damn, it's a pretty sight.

After navigating the traffic of Pittsfield, head north on Route 7. Two miles past Lanesborough you can detour right onto North Main Street and ride an additional nine switchback-rich miles to reach the summit of Mount Greylock. At 3,491 feet, it's the state's highest peak and where a 100-foot-tall war memorial offers a view of five states. If you have neither the time nor the inclination to scale the summit, just keep rolling on Route 7.

By the time you reach New Ashford you're all set for several miles of great elevations and terrific plunges that surround the Brodie Mountain ski area. Farther up the road at Routes 7 and 43, watch for the **Store at Five Corners** (413/458-3176, www.5-corners.com). A general-store anomaly, during its history it's been a tavern, a mustering point for mounted militia, a stagecoach stop, a gas station, a tea room, and a social center. Today, basic staples (thread, detergent, tape) rest beside gourmet groceries, and the market has become an attraction unto itself. No pork rinds in sight, but if you're looking for fine wines, garlic parsley pasta, and other imported fare, you'll find plenty to peruse.

Just a few hundred yards past the Store at Five Corners is the most visually appetizing sight you've seen in a while. Scan the horizon to your right, and the valley looks like a Dalí painting as it melts into low hills a mile away. In fall, the view will prepare you for upcoming scenes of old men in overalls selling pumpkins by the roadside, cornstalks stacked like teepees, and dogs sleeping on the porches of cozy homes. Sunflowers sag under their own weight, and flower gardens speckle yards. The smell of fresh air mingles with the spicy aroma of trees, sweet corn, and smoking chimneys.

Soon you are in Williamstown, a tranquil village built around Williams College (c. 1793). If you're ahead of schedule, take a break downtown where the antiques are pricey and the merchandise is probably available elsewhere. Still, the town is cool, and the **Sterling and Francine Clark Art**

Institute (225 South St., 413/458-9545, www.clarkart.edu, free November–May, $12.50 in summer) is well worth a visit. Even if your walls are hung with paint-by-number masterpieces, you can relive college art appreciation class here, viewing works by artists of the caliber of Sargent, Remington, and Degas. It's open daily except Monday until July 1, then seven days a week through summer.

You know life is good when Route 7 continues north, its steep grades dropping you into the thick of purple and yellow and green hills. The hues reveal that you are entering Vermont, the name derived from the French words *vert* (green) and *mont* (mountain). Within a few miles, you'll notice that something's missing: There are no billboards in Vermont. None. Natural beauty is the state's best advertising. *Trés magnifique.*

Compensating for the lack of billboards, however, are maple syrup sellers. Maple syrup is sold from front porches. Maple syrup is sold from car trunks, at diners, in gas stations, schools, prisons, basements, attics, duck blinds, churches, tollbooths, and bomb shelters. I'd guess that the tidal wave of Vermont maple syrup packaged in jars, jugs, bottles, and canisters will remain long after our sun has flickered out.

As you approach Bennington, you'll certainly notice the 306-foot-tall Bennington Battle Monument. You can see it from 50 miles away, but if you'd like to see it up close, turn left on Main Street (Highway 9) when you hit the center of town. Follow Main Street a short distance to Monument Avenue, where you'll turn right, then right again, taking you to the monument.

When you roll into the north end of Bennington, watch the road signs and veer onto parallel Route 7A. Now you can relax again as you begin your voyage through Vermont. As you approach the village of Arlington, you sense there are no worries here—just mountains to watch and a quiet back road that's coaxing you along. The riding here is sublime and you may never want to stop, but I suggest that you do since you're fast approaching **Snow's Arlington Dairy Bar** (3176 VT Route 7A, 802/375-2546). A favorite with riders, Snow's has been on the ground since 1962, serving hot dogs, chilidogs, fries, and shakes. Pull over, grab a picnic table, and enjoy the surrounding woods. If you carry an AARP card, time your ride for Tuesday's Senior Day and get 10 percent off.

Nine miles later you'll reach Manchester Village, but not without passing hills colored with countless shades of green and bordered by the flowing Batten Kill River. Given the time and desire, you can park your bike and explore the woods and river with full-service **BattenKill Canoe Ltd.** (802/362-2800 or 800/421-5268, www.battenkill.com). It leads tours or turns you loose on the crystal clear, trout-rich waterway that flows beside lonely country lanes and quiet meadows and into deep woods. Although Manchester is a small town, there are other detours to make. To experience 5.2 miles of steep grades and sharp curves, take a scenic ride to the summit of 3,848-foot **Mount Equinox** (802/362-1114, www.equinoxmountain.com, $10), the highest peak in the Taconic Range. The toll road leads to a restaurant, walking trails, and picnic sites, but the Carthusian monastery is off-limits to travelers. Tell 'em you wanna be a monk, and maybe they'll let you in.

Hildene (1005 Hildene Rd., 802/362-1788, www.hildene.org, $12.50), the 24-room Georgian revival mansion once owned by Robert Todd Lincoln (Abe's kid), is on your right off Route 7A. Later home to Lincoln's few descendants, the

Cool Calvin

Calvin Coolidge never did say much, but when he did, you could rest assured he knew what he was talking about. Here's one of Coolidge's comments that's become a favorite inspirational quote:

Nothing in the world can take the place of persistence. Talent will not; nothing is more common than unsuccessful men with talent. Genius will not; unrewarded genius is almost a proverb. Education will not; the world is full of educated derelicts. Persistence and Determination alone are omnipotent. The slogan "Press On" has solved and always will solve the problems of the human race.

house features original furnishings and family effects, as well as formal gardens.

A few miles farther north, the merchants of Manchester Center (est. 1761) tricked out their outlet stores so that wealthy shoppers would think they were getting a good deal. Although outlets no longer mean savings, just try saying that to anyone leaving Polo, Bass, Izod, Calvin Klein, Nautica, Big Dog, or Godiva, and expect to be jerked off your bike and beaten with a sack of size 34 Jordache jeans. Aside from this, with its river, side streets, and non-outlet stores and restaurants, Manchester is well worth a break.

When you leave Manchester, turn right at the roundabout and say *au revoir* to Route 7A and howdy do to Route 11. You've cleared the orgy of outlets and dodged swarms of shoppers, and once again it's just you and the positive strokes that come with traveling by motorcycle. Your bike is scaling the hills northeast of town, and as you enter the Green Mountain National Forest, a scenic pull-off provides a glorious aerial view of Manchester. Since you won't be traveling here in winter, the rising and falling road will give you a chance to practice 1200-cc ski jumps. On any hill, just tap it into neutral, stand on your foot pegs, and stretch forward as you

feel the smooth fall, soft dip at the base, and the slow rise. Feels just like the real thing.

At Londonderry, Route 11 stops, zigs to the left, then introduces you to State Road 100. That's *the* most *righteous* State Road 100. Never before in the history of motorcycling has one road done so much for so many. SR 100 cleaves a path through the center of the Green Mountains and plunges you into the heart of Vermont, where apple trees and general stores and Holstein cows create a new, yet strangely familiar, landscape.

Running toward Ludlow, a riverside ride takes you through wide-open spaces to the junction with Route 155, where you'll veer right to continue on SR 100. In the weeks leading to fall foliage, apple trees are brilliant red, and scattered colors change from dark green to bright red to greenish yellow.

Although Ludlow seems to have seen better days, the Okemo Mountain Ski Resort here offers nice elevations, just as upcoming Tyson provides a pleasing ride beside Echo Lake, which I'm sure is perfectly suitable for swimming when it heats up for a few hours each year. This brings up a point: Sunny, pleasant Vermont can become *Night on Bald Mountain*

© NANCY HOWELL

A simple headstone for a simple man: Calvin Coolidge rests directly across from the small village where he was raised, and where he was sworn into the presidency by his father, a justice of the peace.

in moments. Stow some warm clothes or carry a butane torch in your saddlebags to stave off frostbite.

This is where SR 100 gets interesting. Very. As you near Killington, you'll realize that the ground was laid out by God and the road was probably designed by an engineer who rode an Indian Chief. You'll experience great twists, exhilarating turns, frequent rises, and thrilling drops. The ride gets even more exciting when you turn right to SR 100A.

On the run, you'll see tarpaper shacks with cords of firewood so massive you'd be hard-pressed to tell where the kindling ends and the homes begin. Mountains towering along the roadside are straight from *Land of the Giants*. Don't spare the horsepower as you ride northeast toward Plymouth Notch and the **President Calvin Coolidge State Historic Site** (3780

Rte. 100A, Plymouth, 802/672-3773, www.historicvermont.org/coolidge, $7.50), a turn-of-the-20th-century village preserved in honor of its famous son.

If you doubt that just about anyone can become president, witness this. Coolidge was born on the Fourth of July, 1872 in a sleepy village tucked in the folds of sleepy hills. Even if you don't know a thing about our 30th president, I guarantee you'll spend more time here after you read his observations about government and the United States and learn that he was the last president to write his own speeches. As you tour the village, you may even buy some cheese from the small factory that Calvin's son John operated until he passed away in May 2000. Afterward, take a few minutes at the cemetery across the street. The Coolidge family fronts the road, with Calvin's headstone deservedly marked with the presidential seal.

The SR 100A adventure continues to the junction of Route 4, where you'll turn right for the final 10-mile trip to Woodstock. This winding, level road follows the flow of the Ottauquechee River. Be careful: The curving river can hypnotize, and there's no guardrail. Keep your eyes on the road, and soon you'll be in Woodstock—a most interesting town.

WOODSTOCK PRIMER

If ever a town was sent from Central Casting, it's Woodstock. Everything is here: the church steeple, village green, lazy river, covered bridge, American flags. This is Currier & Ives country.

Woodstock was chartered in 1761 and settled in 1768. The colonial homes, many of which are still standing, were built well and inexpensively using abundant natural materials. Early Woodstock was like a commune, in which bartering replaced cash purchases. Small businesses, including hatters, silversmiths, printers, cabinetmakers, tanners, and jewelers, took up residence in town, while on the outskirts, lumber and sawmills, cider presses, brick kilns, and iron-casting furnaces came into operation.

Self-sufficiency, ingenuity, and humanity are hallmarks of Woodstock's history. Slaves here were freed a century before the Civil War; the earliest Morgan horses were stabled here (as were Jersey cows and Merino sheep); and when farming and industry dropped into the background, America's first ski town was installed here in 1934 and helped make Woodstock a center for tourism. And it still is.

ON THE ROAD: WOODSTOCK

Woodstock is a perfect stop for motorcycle travelers because the roads are right; the beauty is omnipresent; the streets are clinically clean; and great restaurants and neighborhood bars let you kick back after a day on the road.

Only minor flaws exist in this dream state. Woodstock is notorious for its speed traps and some locals grumble that merchants cater too much to wealthy tourists. But more prominent is the fact that Route 4, the road you came in on, is also the primary truck route. Every few minutes, distant rumblings and the squeal of jake brakes announce the arrival of a semi. If you can block out the truck traffic, take solace in simple touches, such as a picture of Calvin Coolidge in a storefront window.

As in Lenox, the town center is best seen on foot, and you'll find plenty of metered parking (and a convenient information booth) at the village square. If the booth is closed, the Woodstock Town Crier on Elm Street is a blackboard on which locals list such newsworthy events as raffles, chicken dinners, hayrides, and garden club meetings. Even the local movie venue—the

Gorgeous gorge: A view from the top of the Ottauquechee Bridge east of Woodstock. It's almost 170 feet to the bottom.

town hall—is a throwback to the 1920s. Even more information is available at the Welcome Center on Mechanic Street, where you can pick up maps of the surrounding area and enjoy what's known as the cleanest bathroom facilities around.

Outstanding shops include the **Village Butcher** (18 Elm St., 802/457-2756), with its few hundred types of wine, cheese, and meat. Here since 1886, **FH Gillingham & Sons** (16 Elm St., 802/457-2100, www.gillinghams.com) remains an old-time general store, selling everything from fresh milk in bottles to hardware, wine, and microbrews. If you're inspired by the scenery and want to learn more about the state, drop by **Pleasant Street Books** (48 Pleasant St., 802/457-4050, www.pleasantstbooks.com), which has two floors filled with more than 10,000 old volumes—from Civil War to travel to Vermonticana. Among them are rare books, first editions, and complete sets.

I'm not sure why, but I think that small towns like this are better viewed after dark. Take some time and walk around after the sun goes down. Though the shops may be closed, you'll have a chance to distance yourself from tourists, pause by the bridge, and watch the Ottauquechee River roll past. Come morning, for a short ride you can join the caravan of bikers on the six-mile run east to **Quechee Gorge**. This is a popular spot for motorcycle travelers and I think that maybe the draw is the 1960s tourist shop that's weighted down with Quechee Gorge spoons, Indian moccasins made in Taiwan, and cedar altars sporting plastic Jesuses. Despite the lack of quality gifts, there's no shortage of tourists ready to buy a geegaw for the breakfast nook in Idaho.

In reality people are here because of the sight of a 168-foot vertical drop below Vermont's oldest steel span bridge. Don't bungee jump—a safer route is the half-mile trail that leads down to the Ottauquechee River. Walking down isn't too bad—smokers do it. Hikers do it, bikers do it, and so do little children. But all are far less enthusiastic about hiking up.

At the bottom, take a break and recline on one of the thousands of wide river rocks. The dry riverbed is a good place to think, as evidenced by all the people writing, sketching, and painting. When you want to ride the road again, farther up Route 4 is the **Quechee Gorge Village,** an old-fashioned shopping plaza that features an antiques center, country store, hypercool diner, and candle shop. When you're done, tie down your plastic Jesus with a bungee and return to Woodstock.

PULL IT OVER:
WOODSTOCK HIGHLIGHTS
Attractions and Adventures

Thankfully, most things worth doing are done outdoors in this pristine countryside. Even though some may seem like grade-school field trips, these excursions are intriguing.

You may scoff that a farm would be of interest, but you haven't yet been to **Billings Farm** (Rte. 12 and River Rd., 802/457-2355, www.billingsfarm.com, $11). This pastoral parcel of land was created to educate the public about the value of responsible agriculture and land stewardship (the passions of lawyer, railroad entrepreneur, and philanthropist Frederick Billings and his wealthy grandson-in-law, Laurance S. Rockefeller). The circa 1871 working farm is a living museum, with guides hosting demonstrations of how they did it in the old days—from rug-hooking to butter-churning to wooden-tool-making. The guides toss out useful data as well: "Count the number of fogs in August, and you can match the number of snows in the winter." Surprisingly fascinating. It's open 10 A.M.–5 P.M. daily May–October, until 3:30 P.M. November–February.

Across the street, the **Marsh-Billings-Rockefeller National Historic Park** (Rte. 12, 802/457-3368, www.nps.gov/mabi, $8, open daily 10 A.M.–5 P.M. June–mid-October), Vermont's first national park, was donated to the United States in 1992 by Frederick Billings's granddaughter, Mary French Rockefeller, and her husband, the late Laurance S. Rockefeller. The park interprets conservation history using the 1870 forest established by Billings as a case study. I highly recommend a guided tour of the family mansion and gardens.

Out toward the Quechee Gorge, the **Simon Pearce Gallery** (1760 Quechee Main St./Rte. 4, Quechee, 802/295-2711, www.simonpearce.com) is open 10 A.M.–9 P.M. daily. While the name suggests a colonial-era factory, this is actually part of a larger chain of glass galleries started by an Irish immigrant in 1981. The timeline doesn't diminish the quality of the work, however. After watching the artists whip a glass out of molten sand, you'll want to raise a glass to their skills. Quality glassware, as well as off-kilter factory seconds, is sold in the gift shop. If your house has settled at a slant, spring for the seconds.

Back in town, locals avoid the megamall googolplex and gather to enjoy movies in a refined setting at the **Town Hall Theatre** (802/457-2620) on the village green. Where else could you watch *Perils of Pauline* in Dolby?

Blue-Plate Specials

Here since 1955, **Wasp's Snack Bar** (57 Pleasant St., 802/457-3334) has diner stools at the counter and eggs, bacon, pancakes, hash browns, and coffee cooking and brewing behind it. You'll have to look for this local hangout, since the signage is minimal. No dinners here, but lunch offers anything the cook can make, plus homemade specials and soups. Nothing fancy, but it's just right.

Homemade "rich super premium" ice cream (served in the basement) is the foundation—as it should be—for **Mountain Creamery** (33 Central St., 802/457-1715). Upstairs, you can eat country breakfasts until 11:30 A.M. and big sandwiches noon–6:30 P.M. If you like your road food sweet, load up on pies, cakes, muffins, cookies, and brownies.

West of the village, on Route 4, is the **White Cottage Snack Bar** (462 Woodstock Rd., 802/457-3455), a *Happy Days*–era roadside diner that draws in tourists and riders who just want a messy hamburger, sloppy chili dog, and a full line of soda fountain treats. Also west of the village, about seven miles away in Bridgewater, is the **Long Trail Brewing Company** (junction of Rtes. 4 and 100A, Bridgewater

Corners, 802/672-5011, www.longtrail.com). Their visitor center is modeled after Munich's Hofbrau Haus and they serve six varieties of microbrews and great pub food, and feature an outdoor deck on the Ottauquechee River. This is a good place to grab lunch and a fresh beer. Watch your speed in Bridgewater—cops patrol it carefully.

Watering Holes

Since 1976, **Bentley's** (3 Elm St., 802/457-3232, www.bentleysrestaurant.com) has been Woodstock's neighborhood bar and, to be fair, restaurant. A few couches, a 1920s style long bar, and creaky wooden floors give this place after-hours appeal. Great lunches and dinners are served, but the microbrews, wines, and casual setting make this spot equally enjoyable for an evening conversation and a good drink—although it often gets wicked busy.

Shut-Eye
Motels and Motor Courts

The large and clean **Shire Motel** (46 Pleasant St., 802/457-2211, www.shire-motel.com, from $98 in summer) has been here since 1963. Situated in the heart of town, it has 42 rooms with all size beds.

A few miles west of town, **Pond Ridge Motel** (506 Rte. 4 W., 802/457-1667, www.pondridgemotel.com, $79–119 high season) offers 13 decent rooms with doubles or queens. If you're staying for a long period of time, consider one of the four rooms with kitchenettes.

Inn-dependence

The **Woodstocker B&B** (61 River St./Rte. 4, 802/457-3896, www.woodstockervt.com, from $110–250) seems like home, with fresh-baked cookies and breads laid out each afternoon. Board games, a whirlpool tub, and killer breakfasts with oven-puffed pancakes add to the effect. This is a great location within walking distance of the village and it has spacious rooms with queen or two double beds—although sounds can carry.

Smack dab on the village green, the largest and most upscale hotel in town, **Woodstock Inn** (14 The Green, 802/457-1100 or 800/448-7900, www.woodstockinn.com, $275 and up in summer), also includes Richardson's Tavern, a restaurant, and premium rooms overlooking a putting green. With 144 rooms, this inn is a popular spot for tourists with deep pockets, and its location and amenities may coax you to join them (if they'll offer an 80 percent discount).

Chain Drive

These chain hotels are in town, or within 10 miles of the city center:

Comfort Inn, Econo Lodge, Hampton Inn, Holiday Inn, Super 8

For more information, including phone numbers and websites, see page 99.

ON THE ROAD: WOODSTOCK TO STOWE

The moment you get home and put your bike in the garage, write a letter to the Vermont highway commissioner and say thanks for the additional 90 miles of SR 100 beyond Woodstock. At the intersection of Routes 4 and 100A South at Bridgewater Corners, you'll find a service station and general store. If you arrived by car, you'd get gas and snacks and leave. But on a bike, you'll want the experience to last. I sat on the porch, read the local bulletin board, watched people buy maple syrup, and enjoyed the reprieve from my routine. You'll have these experiences on the road, too—and often. Take advantage of them.

Routes 100 and 4 are the same for about six miles, and you'll ride north on SR 100 when Route 4 fades away. The road is slow and curving; the idea of a straightaway is foreign in Vermont, which I credit to Vermont's 1964 sale of surplus straightaways to Kansas.

As you swing into satisfying turns, you'll question whether this ride is actually the shortest route between Points A and B. It's not—and that's good. SR 100 rolls through gorgeous farmland, fields, and forest. It rides beside rivers and mountains. And it introduces you to the protectors of the free enterprise system: individuals who live miles from the shadow of a mall and make their living as independent merchants. In the yards of unpainted frame houses and log cabins, signs advertise bread, carved flutes, honey, antiques, artwork, and, of course, maple syrup. This short stretch slowly reveals the diversity of the nation and confirms that this motorcycle tour is a great American adventure.

You'll have little time to contemplate the sensations you feel, because roughly five miles past the split of Routes 4 and 100, you're in the thick of it. South of Pittsfield, you'll see yellow warning signs with the twisting black line that herald a series of quick turns that'll shift your bike beneath you like a hopped-up pendulum. Working the throttle, clutch, and brake in a symphony of shifting makes for a magical experience.

The bucolic nature of Vermont is on display. The roads weave randomly through this countryside, where the rusted edge of tin roofs sag lazily and crumbling mortar flakes off red chimneys. You'll see broken barns and unpainted covered bridges spanning rivers strewn with boulders. The road leads to tight turns and cramped quarters, changes in elevation compensating for monochromatic greenness. Cornfields and farmland don't offer much visual appeal, but if you're not a local, it's strangely satisfying to watch Vermont farmers turn the earth, work the combines, and roll tractors weighted beneath bales of hay.

Depending on its mood and the lay of land, the wide White River will surface on your left or right. With no guardrails to keep you out of the drink, keep one eye on the road and one on the river. The flowing road leads to a small village, the town of Rochester, where it's worth applying the brakes and taking a break. This commercial district is only about two blocks long, but it has everything a motorcyclist needs: a gas station, small market, and the **Rochester Cafe and Country Store** (SR 100, 802/767-4302), which features an old-fashioned soda fountain where you can order breakfast and hot and cold sandwiches.

The ride north from Rochester passes ordinary towns and villages every few miles, but the highlights you'll remember are the long stretches of emptiness. On the sloping roads south of Granville, gravity sucks you into a vortex of trees, leaves, and wild grass until you're completely enveloped by the environment. The Granville Gulf Reservation promises "six miles of natural beauty to be preserved forever." And it delivers. The force of nature is strong here: As you coast downhill, a stream on your right goes uphill. A great waterfall is on your left and it offers a splendid place to stop for a picture and a frigid spray of Vermont water.

The region changes from rural to upper class near Waitsfield. Between here and Morefield is the grandly titled "1800 to 1850 Mad River Valley Rural Historic District." Along with the nice homes and a sense of wilderness, the smell of pine mingles with the scent of stables.

This journey now comes to a close. When you reach SR 100B, Stowe is just 18 miles away. That's 18 more miles of mountains, smooth roads, Vermont farmlands,

and Waterbury—home of Ben & Jerry's, the ice cream capital of the world.

Life is good.

STOWE PRIMER

The village of Stowe lies about six miles southeast of the ski area, and the road north (Route 108) merits a visit as much as the village. Compared to Lenox and Woodstock, there's not much ground to cover here, but motorcycle travelers like going off on a tear along Routes 100 and 108, which intersect at the center of the village.

As far as background, the town was chartered in 1763 and named after descendants of England's Lord Stowe. As far as legend, most people recognize Stowe as a ski resort, although there's actually more of a summer theme in place. When Stowe began a gradual transformation into a resort destination more than a century ago, the main activities were shopping in the village, swimming in swimming holes, and riding up the mountain road to the peak of Mount Mansfield—at 4,393 feet, Vermont's highest point.

That's pretty much what happens today.

ON THE ROAD: STOWE

You've already ridden some of Vermont's best roads on the way up, but if you can't get enough of mountain riding then head north on Route 108 and ride up to Smuggler's Notch. Not only is this a most excellent road for motorcyclists, it was also a favorite route for independent Vermonters who smuggled goods from the United States to Canada during the 1807 Embargo Act. The road proved just as popular for transporting escaped slaves in the 1800s and bootleg liquor during Prohibition. This narrow, isolated road still threads the needle between Mount Mansfield and

Sterling Peak, carved through rock formations created about 400 million years ago. At the summit, you may be able to make out outcroppings like Elephant's Head, Singing Bird, and Smuggler's Face. You may even run across some lost bootleggers.

PULL IT OVER:
STOWE HIGHLIGHTS
Attractions and Adventures

Most of the town's attractions involve natural pursuits. At the **Fly Rod Shop** (2703 Waterbury Rd., 802/253-7346, www.flyrodshop.com), Bob Shannon and staff offer a complete selection of equipment, including locally tied flies and rod and wader rentals. Between May and October, guides can take you to the best fishing spots in the area. But do you have room in your saddlebags for a 20-pound king salmon? Well, do you—punk?

At **Catamount Fishing Adventures** (Barrows Rd., 802/253-8500, www.catamountfishing.com), Willy Dietrich offers four- to eight-hour fly-fishing or spin-fishing excursions in backwoods Vermont. The eight-hour trip includes a free lunch. Trips are based on your level of expertise, so if you normally fish with a shotgun, you're a beginner. Choose from canoe, float tube, small motorboat, or side stream tours in pursuit of trout, bass, and northern pike.

After hugging the road for days at a time, here's a chance to soar like an eagle. Glider rides at **Stowe Soaring** (Morrisville-Stowe State Airport Rte. 100, Morrisville, 802/888-7845 or 800/898-7845, www.stowesoaring.com) range from $99 for 10 minutes to $199 for 40 minutes, with $40/10-minute increments in between. If you've never soared, when the rope pops off the sailplane you'll at first be startled by the lack of engine noise

(none, since there isn't an engine) and then thrilled that the experience feels as freeing as riding your motorcycle. From as much as a mile high, look for the Adirondacks to the west, Jay Peak to the north, Mount Washington to the east, and nothing but air below.

Several hundred years before roads were paved for you and for your bike, Native Americans were cruising the area in their canoes. With rivers and lakes laced across the Green Mountains, you can do the same in a rented kayak or canoe, gliding through farms and forested countryside on the wide and winding Lamoille and Winooski rivers. Three canoe and kayak outfitters are based in Stowe: **AJ's Ski & Sports** (350 Mountain Rd., 802/253-4593 or 800/226-6257, www.ajssports.com); **Umiak Outfitters** (849 S. Main St, 802/253-2317, www.umiak.com); and **Pinnacle Ski & Sports** (3391 Mountain Rd., 802/253-7222, www.pinnacleskisports.com). Since you can't transport a canoe yourself, find where the boats are already in the water. Kayaks rent for about $40 and canoes for about $45 for a full day, with discounts available if you book in advance. Be sure to ask about guided and self-guided river tours.

One of the most popular attractions in the area is located several miles south of Stowe on SR 100 and about a mile north of I-89. It's **Ben & Jerry's** (1281 Waterbury-Stowe Rd., 802/882-1240 or 866/258-6877, www.benjerry.com) and it's pretty interesting. Backed by $5 business diplomas from a correspondence course and a collective life savings of $8,000, in 1978 Ben Cohen and Jerry Greenfield found an abandoned gas station in Burlington and opened an ice-cream parlor. Not only did they vow to use only fresh Vermont ingredients in their ice cream, they also pledged 7.5

percent of pretax profits to employee-led philanthropy. This is the way a business should be run—and the way ice cream should taste. Take the half-hour first-come, first-served tour for $3 and then score some free ice cream hauled up straight from the production line. Beats touring a fertilizer factory.

To walk off the ice cream, when you get back to Stowe put on your walking shoes and set out for a trip past mountains, woods, and farms. The **Stowe Recreation Path** is a 5.5-mile greenway that stretches from Main Street along the West Branch River and Mountain Road to the covered bridge at Brook Road. If you go the distance, keep in mind it'll be another 5.5 miles back. Footnote: The path was named by *Travel + Leisure* as one of the "19 Great Walks of the World."

Blue-Plate Specials

There are absolutely no fast food joints in Stowe, so get ready for some real food. The gathering spot for locals, **McCarthy's** (454 Mountain Rd., 802/253-8626), serves one of the best breakfasts in town. Stick around and chow down on homemade breads, soups, and pie at lunch. The food is cheap and healthy.

At dinnertime, look for **Cactus Cafe** (2160 Mountain Rd./Rte. 108, 802/253-7770, www.cactuscafestowe.com), known as much for its tequilas and 16-ounce handmade margaritas as for its food. Along with Mexican standards (enchiladas, fajitas, quesadillas), are ranch camp ribs and sirloin steaks. If you can't get enough of the great outdoors (who can?), dine in the perennial garden.

If you've got a hankering for wild boar, venison, or pheasant, park it at **Mr. Pickwick's** (433 Mountain Rd., 802/253-7064, www.englandinn.com). It's open daily for lunch and dinner and serves more than 150 varieties of ale, including fresh wheat beer and lambic ales from Belgium. Have a designated rider in your group? Then try one of each. Gotta cigar? Complement it with your choice from the selection of vintage ports, rare cognacs, and single malt scotches.

Watering Holes

In the center of town, **The Whip Bar and Grill** (18 Main St., 802/253-7301, www.greenmountaininn.com) is downstairs at the Green Mountain Inn. Sure, it's a hotel bar, but it feels more like a pub, with its high-back chairs and English riding club design. They serve meals here, and enhance them with great brews.

Gracie's (18 Edson Hill Rd., 802/253-8741) became so popular in a basement bar downtown, that it moved into a much larger location on Edson Road. The new location features a patio, bar, and a menu of burgers, nachos, seafood, and steaks.

At the **Backyard Tavern** (395 Mountain Rd., 802/253-9204) you'll find a basic bar menu with cheeseburgers and chicken fingers, a pool table, a great jukebox, pinball, and $3 draft pints daily.

Try the **Sunset Grille & Tap Room** (140 Cottage Club Rd., 802/253-9281). There's a restaurant here also, but in the Tap Room you can dine on wings, bar pizzas, burgers, and BBQ while watching sports shown on a variety of TVs. Occasionally, the place hosts a cookout on the patio, and pickup horseshoe and volleyball games shape up out back. When you're bored with that, check out the huge domestic beer selection.

Shut-Eye

In the village, **Stowe's Visitor Information Center** (51 Main St., 802/253-7321 or 800/247-8693, www.gostowe.com) also assists travelers with lodging, and there are

40-plus independent inns, hotels, and motels, which offer more than 1,700 rooms. **Stowe Country Homes** (541 South Main St., 802/253-8132, www.stowecountryhomes.com) represents more than a dozen rental cabins, farms, and resorts. If you're traveling with a large group and need a base, check 'em out.

Motels and Motor Courts

After a long day, the **Stowe Inn** (123 Mountain Rd., 802/253-4030 or 800/546-4030, www.stoweinn.com) can make your night. The staff is friendly, the rooms are warm and comforting, and the living room and lounge are designed for a relaxing post-ride conversation. A standard room goes for $99 mid-week and $119 weekends in summer, and the complimentary continental breakfast puts everything over the top.

About 2.5 miles north of the village is the clean and basic **Stowe Motel** (2043 Mountain Rd., 802/253-7629 or 800/829-7629, www.stowemotel.com, $88 and up off-season, $110 and up high season). Sixty rooms and efficiencies are spread between three properties, with king and queen beds at each. Rooms include a continental breakfast.

Inn-dependence

Right in the heart of town, the **Green Mountain Inn** (18 Main St., 802/253-7301 or 800/253-7302, www.greenmountaininn.com, $159 and up high season) is a renovated 1833 home-turned-inn.

It features 81 antiques-filled rooms, 15 suites, 4 efficiencies, and 5 townhomes. The central location and amenities, including a health club, heated outdoor pool, canopy beds, fireplaces, and whirlpool tubs, are just right after the ride. So is the pub. There's a two-night minimum on summer and fall weekends.

After Julie Andrews and Christopher Plummer escaped from the Nazis—no, wait...that was the movie—anyway, after the Von Trapp family left Austria, they wound up in its American counterpart, Stowe, and opened the **Trapp Family Lodge** (Rte. 108—up two miles from town, left at the white church, then two more miles, 802/253-8511 or 800/826-7000, www.trappfamily.com, $245 and up high season). The lodge has sustained itself in large part on the strength of the family's story. Included on the 2,500 acres are 96 rooms in the main lodge with spectacular mountain views, nightly entertainment, a fitness center, three pools, tennis courts, and hiking trails. On Sundays in the summer, there are concerts in the Trapp Family Lodge Concert Meadow, a natural amphitheater. The dining room, lounge, and tearoom feature a European theme.

Chain Drive

These chain hotels are in town, or within 10 miles of the city center:
Clarion
For more information, including phone numbers and websites, see page 99.

Resources for Riders

Berkshires–Central Vermont Run

Massachusetts Travel Information
Massachusetts Road Conditions—617/374-1234
Massachusetts State Park Campgrounds Reservations—877/422-6762,
www.reserveamerica.com
Massachusetts Department of Travel & Tourism—617/973-8500 or
800/227-6277, www.massvacation.com

Vermont Travel Information
Vermont Attractions Association—802/229-4581, www.vtattractions.org
Vermont Campground Association—www.campvermont.com
Vermont Chamber of Commerce—802/223-3443, www.vtchamber.com
Vermont Department of Forests, Parks, and Recreation—802/241-3655 or
888/409-7579, www.vtstateparks.com
Vermont Department of Tourism—802/828-3237 or 800/837-6668,
www.travel-vermont.com
Vermont Fall Foliage Hotline—802/828-3239 or 800/837-6668,
www.vermontfallfoliage.com
Vermont Fish and Wildlife—802/241-3700, www.vtfishandwildlife.com
Vermont Hospitality Council—www.visitvt.com
Vermont Road Conditions—http://511.vermont.gov

Local and Regional Information
Berkshires Visitors Bureau—413/743-4500, www.berkshires.org
Lenox Chamber of Commerce—413/637-3646, www.lenox.org
Stowe Chamber of Commerce—802/253-7321 or 877/467-8693,
www.gostowe.com
Woodstock Chamber of Commerce—802/457-3555 or 888/496-6378,
www.woodstockvt.com

Massachusetts Motorcycle Shops
North's Service—675 Lenox Rd., Lenox, 413/499-3266 or 866/499-3266,
www.northsservice.com
Ronnie's Cycle Sales & Service—150 Howland Ave., Adams, 413/743-0715;
and 501 Wahconah St., Pittsfield, 413/443-0638, www.ronnies.com
RPM's Cycle Sales & Service—326 Merrill Rd., Pittsfield, 413/443-5659

Vermont (and nearby New Hampshire) Motorcycle Shops
Granite State Harley-Davidson—351 Miracle Mile, Lebanon, NH,
603/448-4664, www.granitestateharley.com
Lebanon Motor Sports—63 Evans Dr., Lebanon, NH, 603/448-9434,
www.lebanonmotorsports.com
Ronnie's Cycle Sales & Service—2601 West Rd., Rte. 9, Bennington,
802/447-4606, www.ronnies.com

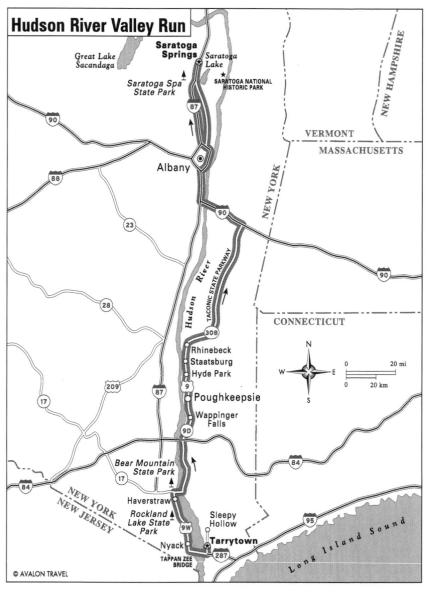

Hudson River Valley Run

Great Lake Sacandaga

Saratoga Springs

Saratoga Lake

Saratoga Spa State Park

★ SARATOGA NATIONAL HISTORIC PARK

Albany

VERMONT

MASSACHUSETTS

NEW HAMPSHIRE

NEW YORK

CONNECTICUT

Hudson River

TACONIC STATE PARKWAY

Rhinebeck
Staatsburg
Hyde Park

Poughkeepsie

Wappinger Falls

Bear Mountain State Park

Haverstraw

Rockland Lake State Park

Sleepy Hollow

Nyack

Tarrytown

TAPPAN ZEE BRIDGE

NEW YORK
NEW JERSEY

Long Island Sound

N W E S

| 0 | 20 mi |
| 0 | 20 km |

© AVALON TRAVEL

Route: Tarrytown to Saratoga Springs via Nyack, Bear Mountain State Park, Hyde Park, Staatsburg, Rhinebeck, Taconic State Parkway

Distance: Approximately 180 miles

First Leg: Tarrytown to Hyde Park (88 miles)

Second Leg: Hyde Park to Saratoga Springs (92 miles)

Helmet Laws: New York requires helmets.

Hudson River Valley Run

Tarrytown, New York to Saratoga Springs, New York

If you've avoided touring New York State because friends convinced you there was nothing here but the traffic of New York City, tune them out, tap your bike into gear, twist the throttle, and head up the Hudson River.

Twenty-five miles north of NYC are the neighboring communities of Tarrytown and Sleepy Hollow, a perfect base from which to begin a tour of the Hudson River Valley. Though close to the capital of capitalism, it's worlds away in texture and feel. You might think you took a wrong turn in Bavaria, but this is indeed America—an America that began more than 150 years before the nation existed. The villages and the following 180 miles will introduce you to a world of distinctive literature, art, history, and cuisine. They will also offer great river roads, hills, scenic vistas, pubs, and diners and lead you into the outstanding Adirondacks.

TARRYTOWN PRIMER

Although Tarrytown looks like an active modern suburb, the sense of history here is omnipresent. In the early 1600s, this area was home to a tribe of the Mohegan family, the Weckquaesgeek. They lived, fished, hunted, and traded along the Pocantico River relatively undisturbed until 1609 when Henry Hudson sailed up the river searching for the northwest passage to India. When he got home he had a technician adjust his GPS system.

Settlers began arriving soon after. The Dutch named the area Slaeperig Haven (Sleepy Harbor) for its sheltered anchorage. Other Dutch settlers arrived, and by 1685, Frederick Philipse owned nearly half of what is now Westchester County. In the 1730s, members of the Livingston family began building riverfront estates, such as Clermont, Wilderstein, and Montgomery Place, all of which are open for tours.

Fast forward to the American Revolution. British soldier/spy John André was captured here, and the papers he was carrying revealed Benedict Arnold's traitorous plan to surrender West Point. A half century later, in 1820, Rip Van Winkle's creator, Washington Irving, drew further attention to the region with the publication of *The Legend of Sleepy Hollow*.

The tranquil area continued to grow. The second half of the 1800s saw freight arrive and depart by river and rail. Factories were built, followed by estates built by the people who built the factories. With the likes of Jay Gould, William Dodge, and John D. and William Rockefeller taking up summer residence, Tarrytown became a destination for the wealthy until the Great Depression, when new income taxes forced many of the *nouveau poore* to give up their estates.

In the mid-1950s, the Tappan Zee Bridge and New York State Thruway were built, opening up the town for commuters. City workers began driving up from NYC and driving up real estate prices. Today, Tarrytown still displays a distinct degree of affluence. So look sharp.

ON THE ROAD: TARRYTOWN

When you arrive in Tarrytown, give yourself a moment to adjust to your surroundings. Couples walk past carrying bags of fresh produce; neighbors stop and pass the time outside antique shops; and merchants thank God they're not working in a mall. You may think you've entered Pleasantville, but you're cruising through one of the oldest villages in America.

Tarrytown's main drag isn't really Main Street but Route 9, the road of choice for buses, trucks, teens, tourists, seniors, and soccer moms hauling vanloads of ball-kicking kids. With all of this traffic buzzing around, it's best to just park your bike and explore on foot. There are several antiques shops and galleries here and if you follow the scents emanating from bakeries, gourmet shops, ethnic restaurants, and coffee bars, you'll eventually arrive in the heart of downtown, which encompasses about six square blocks.

Since Tarrytown is primarily a residential area, amusing diversions are few, but give yourself at least a few hours to roam the streets. The **Sleepy Hollow Tarrytown Chamber of Commerce** (54 Main St., 914/631-1705, www.sleepyhollowchamber.com) is a smart first stop. Located in a narrow building next to the fire station on Main Street, this is where you can score information from the rack of brochures. If something sparks your interest, track it down. If there's little for you here, just consider this the perfect starting line for an extraordinarily full ride.

PULL IT OVER: TARRYTOWN HIGHLIGHTS
Attractions and Adventures

Sometimes, there's a whole lotta shakin' going on at the **Music Hall** (13 Main St., 914/631-3390, www.tarrytownmusichall.org). Built in 1885, this hall is one of the oldest in Westchester County and has hosted over a century of performances by artists like Bruce Springsteen, Chuck Mangione, Tito Puente, Dave Brubeck, Tony Bennett, Judy Collins, Dizzy Gillespie, Lionel Hampton, Lyle Lovett, Wynton Marsalis, Tom Paxton, and Leon Redbone. Folk and classical concerts are performed here as well, and the acoustics are alleged to rival those of Carnegie Hall. If there's a show in town, listen up.

For music of a different sort, head to the banks of the Pocantico River in **Rockefeller State Park Preserve** (Route 117, 1 mile east of Route 9, 914/631-1470, www. friendsrock.org). Washington Irving described it as "one of the quietest places in the whole wide world. A small brook glides through it, with just murmur enough to lull one to repose." If you stow a rod and reel, brown trout are here for catch-and-release fly-fishing, and you can find bass in Swan Lake. Non-resident day licenses (about ten bucks) can be purchased at the park office or Sleepy Hollow Village Hall.

A few miles north of town, you can ride your bike onto an estate to see how the other 0.0001 percent lives. When John D. Rockefeller got tired of living in a dumpy fixer-upper, he had Johnny Jr. build **Kykuit** (pronounced KI-cut, Route 9, entrance at Philipsburg Manor, 914/631-9491, www.hudsonvalley.org), which means "high place." The neoclassical country mansion and gardens, which overlook the Hudson, were completed in 1913 and served as home to four generations of Rockefellers, including Nelson A., who added 20th-century sculptures to the estate's gardens. Vintage carriages and cars (such as a 1918 Crane Simplex) are on display in the Coach Barn, and there's a café on site. It may not be something you've planned to do on a motorcycle tour, but this is a magnificent American estate. Reservations are suggested, with different styles of tours requiring different fees, from $23. Kykuit is open daily except Tuesdays May–October.

When you're in Tarrytown, remember that right next door is Sleepy Hollow. For a road story you'll tell later, retrace the route Ichabod Crane used to flee from the Headless Horseman in *The Legend of Sleepy Hollow*. To duplicate Ichabod's flight, take Route 9 from Patriot's Park (along the old Albany Post Road) to the Sleepy Hollow Bridge under the shadow of the Old Dutch Church. Watch your head.

Shopping

Get within 25 feet of fragrant **Tarrytown Gourmet** (45 Broadway, 914/366-6800) and your schnoz will go into olfactory overdrive. Provisions include fresh pears, mangoes, sweet red plums, olive oil, hot pepper oil, cookies, gourmet pizzas, olives, salami, imported cheeses, candies and cakes, iced drinks, teas, and coffees. Here's a place to get fat and happy and pack up a picnic for the road ahead.

Blue-Plate Specials

Since 1985, **Santa Fe Restaurant** (5 Main St., 914/332-4452, www.santaferestaurant. com) has succeeded by serving Mexican and Southwestern cuisine in the heart of Dutch country. Go figure. Home-cooked without flavor enhancers, all dishes can be spiced to your satisfaction and tolerance for pain. The comfortable neighborhood feel is matched by a full range of Mexican beers and more than 30 premium tequilas. *¡Muy bueno!* The restaurant is open daily for lunch and dinner.

The type of restaurant you look for on a ride, **Horsefeathers** (94 N. Broadway, 914/631-6606) has a pub-style atmosphere with home-style comfort foods like meatloaf, burgers, and mashed potatoes, along with soups, pasta, steaks, and chicken. The big draw is the extensive collection of beers—more than 100 micros—from across the country and around the world. Homey and comfortable, Horsefeathers is open daily for lunch and dinner.

Sunset Cove (238 Green St. at Washington Irving Boat Club, 914/366-7889, www.sunsetcove.net) may have the nicest view on the Hudson. The menu features soups, salads, and sandwiches at lunch, primarily seafood at dinner. The real appeal is the outdoor dining on the river itself—enjoy BBQ and the tiki bar. Pull up a chair on the patio and peer beneath the Tappan Zee Bridge for a view of the New York City skyline 25 miles away. A definite stop for riders.

Shut-Eye

There are few inns in Tarrytown, so if you need to stay the night, you'll probably wind up at one of the chains below—the less expensive options are across the Hudson in Nyack.

Chain Drive

These chain hotels are in town, or within 10 miles of the city center:

Best Western, Comfort Inn, Courtyard by Marriott, Days Inn, Hampton Inn, Hilton, Holiday Inn, Hyatt, La Quinta, Ramada, Residence Inn, Sheraton, Super 8

For more information, including phone numbers and websites, see page 99.

ON THE ROAD: TARRYTOWN TO HYDE PARK

Like John Lennon, New York has a fascination with the number 9. Within a few miles of Tarrytown, you'll discover Route 9, Route 9A, Route 9W, Route 9G, and Route 9D. Right now, head to Route 9W by going west over the Tappan Zee Bridge (aka I-287/I-87/New York State Thruway) into Rockland County, and let the joy begin.

As you roll over the Tappan Zee Bridge, the mighty Hudson River floods past 150 feet below. The setting captured on canvas by 19th-century Hudson River School artists will no longer seem embellished as you begin your ride through a landscape that rivals the magnitude of a Greek epic poem. When you peer downriver to the hazy outline of New York City, you'll picture—if not Odysseus and his crew—then Hudson's ship, the *Half Moon,* under full sail.

A few miles past the bridge, Route 9W branches north off I-287 and heads into the hills. You can decide to ride Route 9 north along the river road past the towns of Nyack and Haverstraw, but a local rider turned me on to a better alternative: By staying on I-287/I-87 and following it northwest, you'll soon be riding along the southern edge of **Harriman State Park**

West Point

I was never in the military, but my mom took me to Marineland once. If you're interested in military history, **West Point** (Route 218, 845/938-2638, www.usma.edu) is worth the six-mile detour north from Bear Mountain State Park. Washington garrisoned his troops here during the Revolutionary War, and in 1802, President Jefferson signed the act of Congress creating the U.S. Military Academy. And that's not all: Lee, Grant, Patton, Eisenhower, and Schwarzkopf all learned to march here.

Since September 11, 2001, it's been more difficult, but not impossible, to gain access to West Point. You can travel onto the post if there's a specific event such as a chapel service, football game, or an event at the performance arts center. Even easier, you can sign up for a tour. Two tours—one an hour, the other two—depart from the Visitors Center and will take you by the Main Cadet Chapel, Trophy Point, and the Parade Field with the longer tour adding the Old Cadet Chapel and West Point Cemetery. To schedule a tour, call 845/446-4724 or visit www.westpointtours.com. If you don't have time for a tour, the Visitors Center, which features a 30-minute movie, is open 9 A.M.–4:45 P.M., and the West Point Museum is right next door.

(845/786-2701). Stay on the road until you reach Route 17 in Sloatsburg and keep an eye out on your right for the entrance to picturesque Seven Lakes Drive. This is a cool, serene, lonely ride through the woods, which reveals, yes, seven lakes— Sebago, Tiorati, Stahahe, Askoti, Cohasset, Kanawaukee, and Skannatati.

This is when you derive the pure pleasure of motorcycling. Feel the fresh air on your skin and in your lungs and listen to the hum of the bike as you ride for miles through the forest and approach a new paradise: **Bear Mountain State Park** (845/786-2701, www.friendsofpalisades. org), a must-see for a high-altitude ride and stunning views of the valley. For motorcycle travelers, the real appeal of the park is ascending Bear Mountain. Passage to the peak comes when you slip off of Seven Lakes Drive and onto Perkins Memorial Drive, a road that introduces another memorable motorcycling moment. Be warned: If you suffer from vertigo, dropsy, or the shakes, don't take this ride since the road twists like your drunken uncle at a wedding reception. While the speed limit is a sensible 25 mph, you could push it to 26 since small boulders have been thoughtfully placed along the road's edge to keep you from going over it. If you take it between summer and the fall foliage season, it is nearly empty and the forest is moist and cool. The downside: On the ride up, sheer drops fall off to your left, and branches and wet leaves can send you skidding. Still, the road is worth the price of admission (free) since you'll be treated to a kaleidoscope of majestic vistas. The beautiful valleys stretched out like long, verdant branches must have been touched by the finger of God. This is America.

When you reach the peak, derive pleasure from the solitude and serenity. An abundance of table-size boulders makes it easy to spread out a picnic, and if you travel off-season or just after a holiday weekend, chances are only a few random travelers will join you.

When it's time to descend, place your bike in neutral and coast; the silence is satisfying. Though it may be slightly dangerous to pull over, do so if there's no traffic behind you—the view of the Hudson River and Bear Mountain Bridge will stay with you forever. The rest of the ride will find you "in the zone" as you begin swinging into corners, diving into short stretches of canopy roads, and cowering beneath boulders looming over the road until you return to Bear Mountain Circle at the confluence of three highways. Right now you're at the circa 1915 Bear Mountain Inn which is worth a stop, if for no other reason than to score a great souvenir picture—its rock and wood construction recalls a Yosemite lodge. Picnic tables, a pool, and Hessian Lake are adjacent to the inn, and there are trails where you can take a walk and think about the ride so far.

From the entrance/exit here, you've come full circle to Route 9W North, which you'll follow toward the Bear Mountain Bridge. Like crossing the Tappan Zee from Tarrytown, crossing east to Route 9D reminds you why you're on a bike. If your timing is right, you may even ride over the speeding Montrealer, the train that slips up the Hudson on the riverside rail between NYC and Canada.

Now you're in Putnam County and on Route 9D (aka the Hudson Greenway Trail) which is a beautiful mountain road that hugs the base of the hills. Passing Phillipstown, the Hudson darts in and out of view nearly as often as the white picket fences, evergreens, and estate homes. The road sticks with the Hudson as you drive north, passing small general stores hawking beer and sandwiches and also a castle on a hill. You may be tempted to speed, but force yourself to relax. You can hurry at work, but when you're traveling…please take your time.

The twists and turns continue into Wappinger Falls, where you'll reach a bridge in the center of town. If you turn left and continue to follow Route 9D, the road is scenic, though not as fast, and eventually leads to your first major commercial center: Poughkeepsie. You, being on a journey of discovery, are not going to settle for this or settle down here. After hooking up with Route 9, keep heading north to your first overnight: Hyde Park.

HYDE PARK PRIMER

Just as fans of Mark Twain trek to Hannibal and worshippers of Donny Osmond pilgrimage to Utah, students of history head to Hyde Park. Along with World War II veterans and Depression-era children who grew up on relief packages, baby boomers, scholars, and foreign tourists whose countries were saved by Franklin Delano Roosevelt arrive to pay their respects to the 32nd president, whose home and gravesite are located here.

Most of us have heard of Hyde Park, so it's a bonus that it turns out to be a perfect place to rest your bike, stay the night, enjoy a decent meal, and get an education. In 1705, New York provincial governor Edward Hyde presented this parcel of land to his secretary, Peter Fuconnier. Hyde's munificence earned him a namesake estate and, later, a namesake town, established in 1821. Mills sprang up on Hudson River tributaries, and, by the turn of the 20th century, Roosevelts, Vanderbilts, and other wealthy families began settling in.

ON THE ROAD: HYDE PARK

Sorry, there is no true commercial district within Hyde Park—and that's one of its assets. The town rests along a straightaway highlighted with a handful of attractions, so take it for what it is: a quiet and historically significant stop between Tarrytown and Saratoga Springs.

PULL IT OVER: HYDE PARK HIGHLIGHTS
Attractions and Adventures

If FDR had never achieved national prominence, you may never have heard of Hyde Park. But he did, and today the **FDR National Historic Site** (4079 Albany Post Rd./Rte. 9, 845/229-9115 for headquarters or 800/337-8474, www.nps.gov/hofr) is a shrine for those who want to see how this pastoral countryside helped shape an extraordinary man. With the exception of 13 years in Washington and a few more in Albany, FDR spent his entire life here. This is also his resting place; he and Eleanor are buried in a rose garden adjacent to the house. Unless you arrive with the NPS America the Beautiful Pass, admission is $14 for the house and museum tour, $7 for the FDR museum alone.

The tour starts in the visitors center where, if you're not familiar with the arc of his life, a 22-minute film, *A Rendezvous With History,* will prepare you for what's to come. His home, once known as Springwood, is filled with original books, china, paintings, furniture, and an old kitchen chair modified slightly by FDR himself—with the addition of wheels, it became his favorite wheelchair. In the **FDR Presidential Library and Museum** (the first presidential museum ever built), the desk demands special attention. It's just as it was on the day he died in April 1945. Motorcyclists may get a kick out of the 1938 Ford Phaeton shown in the basement. It's equipped with manual controls for the disabled president. After hours spent roaming the estate, however, I found the most

Art of the Valley

If you experience a sense of déjà vu along the Hudson, you may have seen it before...During the 1800s, popular imagination considered the Hudson to be the American Rhine, and its imposing country estates surely rivaled those of the German river or the chateaux of the French Loire district. Frederick Church and fellow artists captured this prevailing sentiment in an art movement called the Hudson River School. Images of the trees and lakes, waterfalls and rivers of the Hudson and Catskill Mountains were adorned with Grecian temples and sweeping panoramas. As you ride through the valley, the essence of those images will reappear time and again—minus the Grecian temples.

intriguing and touching displays were the letters and gifts the president received from average Americans expressing gratitude for the relief programs that put them back to work. The site is open 9 A.M.–5 P.M. daily.

You can't think of Franklin without thinking of his wife Eleanor, the woman he referred to as his "legs and eyes" since she was ready and able to go where he couldn't—from coal mines to the front lines—and report back on issues of importance. Still, FDR and his mother froze Eleanor out of their world and the tacit agreement was that Eleanor would reside a few miles away at Val-Kill (Stone Cottage). Established as a furniture factory to provide work to local artisans, Val-Kill served as Eleanor's retreat from 1926 until 1945. After FDR died, it became her primary residence and a gathering place for world leaders, including Churchill, JFK, Krushchev, Nehru, and Marshall Tito (who left the Jackson Five to lead Yugoslavia). **Val-Kill** (Rte. 9G, 800/337-8474, www.nps.gov/elro, $8) now serves as the Eleanor Roosevelt National Historic Site. It's open 9 A.M.–5 P.M. daily in summer, 9 A.M.–5 P.M. Thursday–Monday off-season.

Nobody muttered, "there goes the neighborhood" when the Vanderbilts moved to town. **Vanderbilt Mansion** (Rte. 9, 845/229-7770, www.nps.gov/vama, $8) reflects that family's obsession with building homes large enough to drain the kids' inheritance. This Beaux-Arts mansion was the home of Louise and publicity-shy Frederick, who, like myself, was recognized primarily for being a splendid yachtsman, a gentleman farmer, and an "unassuming philanthropist." Louise died in 1926 and Freddy in 1938, and Louise's niece inherited the property a year before she told her neighbor (FDR) that she was donating it to the nation. As you leave the grounds, on your left is an overlook with a tremendous view of the mighty Hudson. The home is open 9 A.M.–5 P.M. daily, December–April.

In Hyde Park, the CIA isn't educating double naught spies. Here, the CIA is the **Culinary Institute of America** (845/471-6608, www.ciachef.edu). Down the road on Route 9, it is the only residential college in the world devoted entirely to culinary education. Founded in 1946 in New Haven, Connecticut, the school moved into this turn-of-the-20th-century former Jesuit seminary in 1972. Today, college-age apprentice chefs, servers, and maître d's at the 150-acre campus are—surprisingly—studying alongside doctors, lawyers, and stockbrokers who dropped out of their careers to do something fun. You may see the campus when you drop in to eat, although one-hour tours (845/451-1588, $5) conducted by students are available 10 A.M. and/or 4 P.M. on Mondays, Wednesdays, and Thursdays.

If your alter-ego is an angler and you want to catch your own meal, the river, streams, ponds, and creeks here are well-stocked with rainbow, brook, and brown trout, as well as bluegills, sunfish, bullhead, rock bass, and small and large striper. For guide services, check out **Hudson Valley Angler** (Red Hook, 845/758-9203, www.hudsonvalleyangler.com).

Blue-Plate Specials

If this is a once-in-a-lifetime ride, consider a once-in-a-lifetime dining experience. The aforementioned **Culinary Institute of America** (Rte. 9, 845/471-6608 for reservations, www.ciachef.edu) features four student-staffed restaurants and a bakery that open to the public. If you travel with appropriate dress in your saddlebags, take a break from the roadside diners and enjoy a classic meal at the American Bounty (regional and seasonal), St. Andrew's Cafe (casual contemporary à la carte), Escoffier (French cuisine), or Caterina de Medici (fine Italian). Prices are slightly lower than they will be when your CIA chef begins working for a five-star restaurant a few weeks hence. The restaurants are closed the first three weeks of July, December 20–January 5, and some holidays.

The retro 1930s American diner decor is right on target at **Eveready Diner** (Rte. 9, 845/229-8100, www.theevereadydiner.com), and so is the menu for motorcycle travelers. Pull up here and order from a menu featuring soups, burgers, and daily specials (the beef stew is great on a cold day). The diner is open 24 hours Friday and Saturday, 5 A.M.–1 A.M. weekdays.

An inspiring American tale is revealed at **Coppola's** (Rte. 9, 845/229-9113), where an immigrant family arrived in 1954, grew dissatisfied as dishwashers, and opened their first local restaurant in 1961. Now there are three restaurants run by the family's second generation. This is traditional Italian cuisine, with extraordinary veal parmigiana, penne à la gorgonzola, and seafood specials served indoors or on the deck.

Watering Holes

In 1933 as he signed the bill ending Prohibition, FDR was quoted as saying, "I think this would be a good time for a beer." Six decades later, some locals at the **Hyde Park Brewing Company** (4076 Albany Post Rd., 845/229-8277, www.hydeparkbrewing.com) took up the cause in this microbrewery across from Roosevelt's birthplace. One of Hyde Park's rare nightspots to boast a full bar and live music, the pub serves six beers (including Rough Rider Red Lager and Von Schtupp's Black Lager)—all brewed right here. The pub is open daily.

Sports fans and Irishmen hang out 'til the wee hours at **Darby O'Gill's** (3969 Albany Post Rd., 845/229-6662). It's open daily, or maybe I should say nightly, since closing time isn't until 4 A.M. Along with beer and mixed drink specials, there are massive high-def televisions.

Shut-Eye

The choices of lodging in Hyde Park range from motels to…motels. Contact the Chamber for a complete list, or to find larger inns and chains, backtrack to Poughkeepsie.

Motels and Motor Courts

The same family that runs Coppola's restaurant also runs the **Village Square Country Inn** (4167 Albany Post Rd., 229/7141, www.coppolas.net, $70 and up), which has 22 rooms, an outdoor pool, and provides a continental breakfast. Otherwise, the **Roosevelt Inn** (4360 Albany Post Rd., 845/229-2443, www.roosevelt-innofhydepark.com, $70–135) is a good, old-fashioned American motel. Try one of 25 clean rooms, some with king beds and some with fridges. Get off to a good start at the retro coffee shop, serving breakfast 7–11 A.M. The **Quality Inn** (4142 Albany Post Rd., 845/229-0088, $60 and up) is clean and cheap. Along with its 61 basic economy rooms, it tosses in a continental breakfast, cable TV, and a clerk on duty 'round the clock.

Inn-dependence

If you have an urge to splurge, stay at the **Belvedere Mansion** (10 Old Rte. 9, Staatsburg, 845/889-8000, www.belvederemansion.com, $225 and up), where the hillside setting at this spa-turned-inn offers a great view of the Hudson. The first floor of the main house is a restaurant (as well as a handy pub) and the upstairs features six rooms adorned with 18th-century French antiques and trompe l'oeil cloud-painted ceilings. Riders who share my budget may opt to bunk down in the converted stable, which is now a row of reasonably priced rooms ($95 and up) featuring queen beds, private baths, and a patio. The gravel driveway is a nuisance for kickstands, but if you're riding solo, a single concrete slab will hold your bike.

Chain Drive

These chain hotels are in town, or within 10 miles of the city center: **Econo Lodge, Quality Inn, Rodeway**

For more information, including phone numbers and websites, see page 99.

ON THE ROAD: HYDE PARK TO SARATOGA SPRINGS

Leaving Hyde Park, the two-lane road begins with some slow curves accented by stands of pines. The village itself—just a few stores and shops—can be bypassed to embark on the next leg of your journey. Although there are no identifiable signs, from here to Germantown in neighboring Columbia County, you'll be riding through the Mid-Hudson Valley, a 32-square-mile area recognized by the Department of the Interior as a National Historic Landmark District.

Miles north, you'll cruise through the village of Rhinebeck, which—midway between Albany and New York—was a logical stop for commercial river and road traffic. At the corner of Route 9 and East Market Street (Rte. 308) is the intersection of the old King's Highway and Sepasco Indian Trail. On your left is the circa 1766 **Beekman Arms** (845/876-7077, www.beekmandelamaterinn.com) which boasts that it's the oldest inn in America. Although you'll find a few hundred other "oldest inns" around the country, "The Beek" gets points for hosting George Washington, Benjamin Harrison, and FDR—who wrapped up each gubernatorial and presidential campaign with a front-porch speech. In 1775, this was the Bogardus Tavern, a bar that stayed open while the Fourth Regiment of the Continental Army drilled on its front lawn before the war. If you're tired enough to stop, but not tired enough to stay the night, kick back with an ale in the warm, rich setting of the Colonial Tap Room.

If your schedule allows, take Route 9 north, detour onto Stone Church

Road, and head to the **Old Rhinebeck Aerodrome** (9 Norton Rd., Red Hook, 914/752-3200, www.oldrhinebeck.org), an antique aircraft museum that displays World War I and Lindbergh-era aircraft such as a 1917 Fokker DR-1 tri-plane, a 1915 Newport 11, and a 1918 Curtiss-Jenny, along with old cars and vintage motorcycles including several Indians, a 1913 Excelsior, 1909 Merkel Light, and a 1916 Royal Enfield with sidecar. At 2 P.M. mid-June–October Saturdays and Sundays, it also presents a flying circus reminiscent of the Great Waldo Pepper. If you're ready to get off the bike, drop $65 bucks and climb into a 1929 open cockpit biplane for a 15-minute barnstorming ride. The aerodrome is open 10 A.M.–5 P.M. daily mid-May–late October. Admission costs $10 Monday–Friday, $20 for the weekend air show.

If there's time to spare, Routes 9G and 9J roughly follow the Hudson all the way to Albany. If time is tight, turn right onto East Market Street (Rte. 308) just past the Beekman Arms and motor past splendid examples of Italianate revival homes and Victorian architecture. If you've spent the morning in Hyde Park, it may be afternoon as you head east—so as the sun settles over the Hudson, you'll feel the warmth on your back and smell the scent of the forest as you cruise down the road. Long shadows fall before your bike, and Little Wappinger Creek occasionally skims into view. In the early fall, acres of harvested cornfields accent the landscape, and the country ride becomes distinguished by its even, level serenity. Six miles after you turn onto Route 308 in a lazy loop toward Rock City, the road becomes Route 199.

The pleasure of cruising through four more miles of farmland will adjust your attitude and prepare you to ride one of the most beautiful roads in America. The Taconic State Parkway (TSP) cautions it is for "passenger cars only," but the sign is obviously the work of some corrupt anti-motorcycle administration. Rest assured that motorcycles are allowed.

Even if you forsake river views, the road is faster and less congested than Route 9. The result is that you'll enjoy a ride that acknowledges that life may be short, but it can be big.

The road is so pristine that the sweeps and dips and gentle drops affirm your existence. The cool air and sweet smell of your surroundings are only part of the adventure. You'll drop close to a hundred feet in less than a mile; you'll encounter stunning views and roadside wildflowers, black ash, slippery elm, arrowwood. Scenic overlooks punctuate the parkway. Look for one in Columbia County where the historic Livingston Manor stood, once the focal point of a 160,000-acre estate along the Hudson River.

Just as you pass over Routes 2 and 7, past the signs for Ancram and Taghkanic, the view will not only knock your socks off, but your boots may fly, too. On a clear day, at least 50 miles of rolling hills unfold to the horizon and possibly to the next galaxy. The view is yours. Use it.

Mea culpa: If I didn't have to take you on the following roads, I wouldn't. The TSP connects with I-90 and, to make time through Albany, you'll be shoved onto I-87. The switch from pastoral scenes to six lanes of fast, tense traffic will change your karma in an instant. The antidote is clearing Albany and finding Route 9 once again. While it's not as picturesque as its counterpart further south, it does clear up near a neat little town called Round Lake (which is worth a quick look) and will calm you down until you reach my favorite American city, Saratoga Springs.

SARATOGA SPRINGS PRIMER

For a long stretch, many towns across the nation inexplicably opted to clear out their historic districts and place their bets on strip malls. In Saratoga Springs, they decided to put more than a thousand buildings on the National Register of Historic Places. The result is—if this makes sense—the town is so real it looks fake.

Broadway, the town's main boulevard, is an artifact that gains the most attention. When Gideon Putnam laid out the 120-foot wide thoroughfare in the early 1800s, he did it to ensure that a team of four horses could make a U-turn. The wide avenue and broad sidewalk make this the most enjoyable street in the nation for walking, riding, or enjoying a libation at a neighborhood bar. Farther up Route 9, you can ease away the kinks of the ride by dropping into a mineral bath at 2,200-acre **Saratoga Spa State Park** (S. Broadway, 518/584-2535, www.saratogaspastatepark. org).

The baths are still here because, in the early 1900s, this was the place to "take the waters." Now it's the place to kick back after a day on the road. Salty waters from ancient seas are trapped beneath limestone layers and sealed by a solid layer of shale. Because the Saratoga Fault zigzags beneath the town, it releases water made bubbly by carbon dioxide gas. Local Iroquois Indians knew well before the 1700s that minerals entering the water also added to the spring's therapeutic value.

Although Saratoga had earned its historical stripes in the Revolution ("Gentleman Johnny" Burgoyne surrendered his Crown Forces nearby on October 10, 1777), it was during the Civil War that John Morrissey, a street fighter who had been indicted twice for burglary, once for assault, and once more for assault with intent to kill, channeled his destructive energies into a horse-racing track. His gamble worked, and by the turn of the 20th century, the Saratoga Race Track complemented his Saratoga casinos.

Although reform politicians later closed the track, it quickly reopened through a loophole and its fortunes rose and fell until well after World War II when the New York Racing Association formed. That's when the focus of the track changed from mere gambling to the love of horse racing. Today with the track drawing summer visitors and the spas providing warm relief year-round, Saratoga is still in the running.

ON THE ROAD: SARATOGA SPRINGS

One of the fringe benefits of a good motorcycle tour is rolling into a town that would make a perfect vignette in a Mark Twain novel or Charles Kuralt feature. Saratoga Springs is one of those places. Even when the ponies aren't racing on America's oldest track, Saratoga is a must-see.

Within blocks of Broadway, you'll find side streets dotted with cool shops. In Congress Park there are wide lawns and a sculpture by Daniel Chester French (of Lincoln Memorial fame). Around town are slices of Americana that will make you wonder if you've wandered onto the set of *It's a Wonderful Life*.

Sometimes I wonder. Each time I ride here I get the sense that this town is strangely like Bedford Falls. When you pass the stunning Adirondack Trust at Broadway and Lake, you expect to peer in at Mr. Potter counting George Bailey's bankroll. As you walk or ride the avenue, the preserved architecture, liveliness of the street, and pleasant look on townspeople's faces as they actually shop along the main street is emotionally powerful and thoroughly satisfying.

Two streets in particular are worth exploring by bike. Head toward Skidmore College on North Broadway and you'll view grand homes reflecting architecture from the Greek Revival, Arts and Crafts, and postmodern periods. The second is Union Avenue, a broad boulevard bordered by palatial homes accented with gazebos, Gothic gables, gingerbread trim, and stained-glass windows.

For any tour—on foot or on your bike—swing by the Visitors Center in **Drink Hall** (297 Broadway) and pick up maps and a fact-filled brochure titled "Strolling Through Saratoga Springs" which suggests five walking tours that will acquaint you with the very best of what this town has to offer.

PULL IT OVER: SARATOGA HIGHLIGHTS
Attractions and Adventures

Where else can you sit back and bet on thoroughbreds shaking the ground from just 10 feet away? And all for three bucks! Don't pass up a visit to the **Saratoga Race Course** (Union Ave., 518/584-6200 in July and August or 718/641-4700 off-season, www.nyra.com/saratoga). The "sport of kings" is held at America's oldest racetrack, and the sense of tradition here is omnipresent. From the swells in the box seats to the two-bit bettors clenching their tickets trackside, this spectacle guarantees a good time. The racing season lasts slightly more than 30 days in July and August, so if you insist on competing with van-driving tourists during peak season, be sure to reserve one morning for "Breakfast at the Track," and stick around for the famed Travers Stakes in August. The track is closed Tuesdays.

After a hard day's ride—hell, even after an easy day's ride—**Congress Park** on Broadway is therapeutic. The turn-of-the-20th-century setting is enhanced by the Canfield Casino, once a favorite hangout of larger-than-life Diamond Jim Brady. Numerous quiet spots beckon you to stretch out on the lawn and enjoy nature. Settle back and listen to the groundskeepers manicure the grounds and watch geese overhead slicing their way south. You'll find another peaceful place by the Daniel Chester French statue erected in memory of Spencer Trask, a man, says the inscription, whose "one object in life was to do right and observe his fellow man. He gave himself abundantly to hasten the coming of a new and better day." Not a bad legacy, Spence.

After the racetrack, Congress Park, and Broadway's shops and pubs, take time to explore **Saratoga Spa State Park** (S. Broadway, 518/584-2535). Within its 2,000-plus acres are 18- and 9-hole golf courses (518/584-2008), the Gideon Putnam Resort & Spa (24 Gideon Putnam Rd., 518/584-3000 or 800/732-1560), a performing arts center (518/587-3330), and the circa 1930s Roosevelt Baths & Spa (37–39 Roosevelt Dr., 518/226-4790). Just a mile south of town, this is a perfect short run. Riding south down Broadway, take a right and enter the Avenue of the Pines, a picturesque road that leads to the Gideon Putnam Resort. Later, ride the Loop Road past Geyser Creek into the heart of the park.

In addition to watching the ponies, another popular outdoor activity is hanging out at Saratoga Lake, just four miles from the city center. Ride Route 9 South (Union Ave.) to Route 9P South and head over the bridge. The eight-mile-long lake is great for sailing, rowing, bass fishing, and waterskiing and several small restaurants have sport decks where you can pull over to enjoy a sandwich and a beer while looking out over the lake. To get out on the

Americade Motorcycle Rally

A late arrival to the rally circuit, the first "Cade" hit the road in May 1983. Originally called "Aspencade" after a New Mexico rally that celebrated the changing colors of the aspen, "Aspencade East" was hosted by veteran motorcyclist Bill Dutcher at the resort community of Lake George, New York, and attracted more than 2,000 attendees. To distance itself from typical rallies, this event stressed that it was "not the place for shows of speed, hostile attitudes, or illegally loud pipes."

In 1986, the name was changed to reflect the multi-brand, national-sized rally it had become. **Americade** (518/798-7888, www.tourexpo.com) is now the world's largest touring-focused event. Some of this is thanks to the Tour Expo tradeshow that's a big part of the event, as are mini-tours, self-guided tours, seminars, social events, and field events. Perhaps its greatest advantage is its location. Americade takes place at the southern gateway to the 6.1 million acre Adirondack Park, a preserve which is larger than Yellowstone, Glacier, Smokey Mountain, Yosemite, and Olympic National Parks *combined*. Ride slowly and take pleasure in its 2,800 lakes and ponds, 30,000 miles of rivers and streams, and 43 mountains with elevations over 4,000 feet.

water, you can rent a fishing or pontoon boat at the **Saratoga Boatworks** (549 Union Ave./Rte. 9P, 518/584-2628, www.saratogaboatworks.com), while **Point Breeze Marina** (1459 Rte. 9P, 518/587-3397, www.pointbreezemarina.com), Saratoga's largest marina, rents pontoons, speedboats, fishing boats, and canoes. You can find gear, bait, and tackle at shops near the marinas.

Saratoga National Historical Park (648 Rte. 32, Stillwater, 518/664-9821, www.nps.gov/sara, $3) is a must-see. Before the battles of Saratoga on September 19 and October 7, 1777, few colonists felt certain that their ragtag army and militias could forge America into an independent country. But after General John Burgoyne surrendered his 6,000 British soldiers to General Horatio Gates on October 17, the American Revolution had reached a turning point and it was only a matter of time before Gates's colleague Washington would drive things home. The dioramas, exhibits, films, and 10-mile battlefield tour road are emotional reminders of America's quest to be free. The park is open 9 A.M.–5 P.M. daily, April–mid-November.

Civil War buffs may be familiar with the name Mount McGregor. To provide for his family, a dying Ulysses S. Grant lived here while completing his memoirs. The catch is that had Grant not died here, the **Ulysses S. Grant Cottage** (518/587-8277, www.grantcottage.org, $4) would have been torn down to make room for the adjacent prison. Ignore the shouts of the cons and enjoy the steep ride to the peak. Take Route 9 North left onto Corinth Mountain Road, and then take a quick right and follow signs to Grant Cottage. Hours are iffy and it's only open in the summer. Call in advance.

If you're thrilled by thoroughbreds like Man o' War, Secretariat, and Seabiscuit, then it's a given that you should head to the **National Museum of Racing and Hall of Fame** (Union Ave. across from Saratoga Race Course, 518/584-0400, www.racingmuseum.org, $7). Open daily, the museum's films, special exhibits, equine art, and miniature wax figurines of jockeys (at least I *thought* they were miniatures) tell the story of horse racing. Kick in an extra three bucks for the Oklahoma Track Tour, an early morning behind-the-scenes tour of stables, the backstretch, and the area where grooms prepare horses for the race. Pony up an extra five bucks and experience the thrill of seeing what it's like to ride a racehorse. Sitting astride a mechanical horse and watching visuals gathered by a "jockey-cam," you go through three races: a warm-up, out of the training gate, and then into a real race to see and feel the perspective, adrenaline, and sensation of the real thing.

Sure, it seems cheesy riding a trolley after getting off your bike, but the information shared by the drivers/historians of **Trolley Tours** (518/584-3255) will spike your learning curve. And for only a $1.50! Trolleys run 10 A.M.–8:30 P.M. Tuesday–Sunday July–Labor Day, departing from the visitors center and various stops along Broadway.

At some point you may wind up at the **Saratoga Performing Arts Center** (Saratoga Spa State Park, S. Broadway, 518/587-3330, www.spac.org) for an outdoor concert by artists like James Taylor, Bruce Springsteen, and the Dave Matthews Band (as well as the Philadelphia Orchestra and New York City Ballet). Then, finally, reward yourself with a taste of indulgence. What takes place at the **Roosevelt Baths & Spa** (37–39 Roosevelt Dr., Saratoga Spa State Park, 518/226-4790) may sound like punishment for Cool Hand Luke, but Lordy! does it feel good after a ride. In this old-fashioned spa, you can get wrapped up in hot sheets, have someone squeeze the tightness out of your muscles, then plunge into steamy, sweat-inducing water…paradise. Prices range from $25 for a mineral bath to $85 for a one-hour massage. Hours vary by season; call in advance. Note: If the Roosevelt's closed and you gotta have someone rub you the right way, call on the affordable **Crystal Spa** (120 S. Broadway, 518/584-2556, www.thecrystalspa.net) which is open year-round.

Shopping

Normally I wouldn't recommend a souvenir store, but Saratoga Springs is such an incredible town it's worth a memento or two. One place to find some great horse and racing prints is at **Impressions of Saratoga** (368 Broadway, 518/587-0666, www.impressionssaratoga.com), and there are some fantastic new, used, and vintage guitars and smaller instruments for making music on the road over at **Saratoga Guitar** (438 Broadway, 518/581-1604, www.saratogaguitar.com). If Elvis could ride his Honda 350 and carry a guitar in *Roustabout,* you have the right to do the same.

On a long tour, one of the greatest pleasures is escaping routine and digging into a good book. You'll find a ton of them within a vacated bank vault at **Lyrical Ballad Bookstore** (7 Phila St., 518/584-8779). One of the finest used and rare bookstores I've seen, it's brimming with 100,000 editions, which means there are more topics here than in a year's worth of Oprah. The bookstore is open 10 A.M.–6 P.M. Monday–Saturday, 11 A.M.–6 P.M. Sunday.

Gotta jones for a stogie? **Smokin' Sam's Cigar Shop** (5 Caroline St., 518/587-6450) is open until midnight in season.

You don't have to travel to Palm Beach to watch pony boys whacking the ball; they've been doing it around here since 1898. If you're here between July and Labor Day, cruise over to **Saratoga Polo** (518/584-8108, www.saratogapolo.com, $25) to watch the world's top polo players get a "chukker" going. Granted, it's ritzy, but the action's fast and furious—even more so when I rode my bike on the field.

Blue-Plate Specials

Compton's Restaurant (457 Broadway, 518/584-9632) opens daily for breakfast (served all day) and lunch. This diner isn't old-fashioned, it's just really old. You wanted an early start? Breakfast begins at 4 A.M. on weekdays and 3 A.M. on weekends. Inhale two eggs, home fries, toast, and coffee, plus ham, bacon, sausage, or hash—all for about five bucks.

Traditional Southern food is hard to find even in the South these days, but **Hattie's** (45 Phila St., 518/584-4790, www.hattiesrestaurant.com) has been serving Louisiana cuisine like fried chicken, ribs, catfish, pork chops, and homemade desserts since 1938. If you can't tour south of the Mason-Dixon, grab a table here. In season, Hattie's is open seven days a week for breakfast, lunch, and dinner, and off-season for dinner Wednesday–Sunday. Enjoy the full bar and outdoor revelry on the patio in the summer.

The **Saratoga Diner** (153 S. Broadway, 518/584-4044) has been known to locals and diners since 1948. The lunch specials include soup, an entree (pork chops, stuffed peppers, turkey), and dessert. They're open 6 A.M.–midnight and 24 hours on the weekends.

Watering Holes

Opened in 1970, **Saratoga Tin & Lint Company** (2 Caroline St., 518/587-5897) is Saratoga's quintessential neighborhood bar. In a basement setting complete with low ceilings, Tin & Lint features creature comforts like wooden benches and one of the best jukeboxes on the road. If you need more convincing, keep in mind that Soupy Sales—*the* Soupy Sales—downed a brew or two here once. You can buy pints of ale for $3 and pitchers for $7 until 4 A.M. daily.

The Parting Glass (40–42 Lake Ave., 518/583-1916, www.partingglasspub. com) is an Irish pub serving affordable pub-style food, all of which can be washed down by your choice of 100 bottled beers or 36 beers on tap. The pub features live Irish and American folk music, darts, and shuffleboard. For a more tranquil evening, **Gaffney's** (16 Caroline St., 518/587-7359, www.gaffneysrestaurant.com) is primarily a restaurant, although one that offers lots of locals as well as knowledgeable travelers a quiet place to listen to a variety of music (rock, jazz, blues) with a cold beer or a bottle of wine.

Shut-Eye

Numerous independent motel/spas line Broadway, the majority of them clean and tidy. Motels are great when traveling by bike; just park right out front. If you arrive in racing season, ouch! You'd better win a lot of cash: Rates can more than double and some places may expect three-night minimums.

Motels and Motor Courts

Smack dab in the middle of everything is the plain Jane **Saratoga Downtowner Motel** (413 Broadway, 518/584-6160 or 888/480-6160, www.saratogadowntowner. com, $89 and up off-season, $239 and up race season). It has 42 AAA rooms, continental breakfast, and—get this—an indoor pool beneath a retractable roof that opens in the summer. The **Springs Motel** (189 Broadway, 518/584-6336, www. springsmotel.com, $95 off-season, $195 race season) is near the racetrack and the state park. It has 28 spacious and clean rooms.

Inn-dependence

In its early days as a resort town, Saratoga Springs created some notable inns and hotels. One of the finest is the **Adelphi Hotel** (365 Broadway, 518/587-4688, www.adelphihotel.com, $130 and up shoulder season, $255 and up race season), not only because of its grandeur, but because of the subtle anachronisms captured in the blend of 1920s art deco style and tropical casualness. The 34 rooms boast high ceilings, private baths, and a far-from-generic decor. The day gets off to a perfect start with breakfast on the verandah and wraps up in one of the coolest lobby bars you'll find. This is the premier spot to relax and relive the 1920s, whether you're passed out under the palms or sampling a cocktail, beer, or daiquiri in the faux-painted bar.

Kathleen and Noel Smith are two of the friendliest people running one of the nicest inns in Saratoga. **Saratoga Arms** (495 Broadway, 518/584-1775, www.saratogaarms.com, $195 and up off-season, $350 and up race season) offers large, comfortable rooms right on Broadway and within walking distance of the action.

For a more natural and cost-effective setting, stay at the **Saratoga B&B** (434 Church St./Rte. 9N, 518/584-0920, $109–239, www.saratogabnb.com) and adjacent **Saratoga Motel** (440 Church St.,

518/584-0920, www.saratogabandb.com, $79–149). Both sit on five wooded acres a few miles up Route 9N and are popular with riders for the motel setting and lower rates.

Chain Drive

These chain hotels are in town, or within 10 miles of the city center: **Best Western, Comfort Inn, Courtyard by Marriott, Hampton Inn, Hilton, Holiday Inn, Residence Inn, Sheraton** For more information, including phone numbers and websites, see page 99.

SIDE TRIP: ADIRONDACKS

Just because this ride ends at Saratoga Springs, it doesn't mean yours has to. Just north of Saratoga, **Americade** (www. tourexpo.com), the world's largest tour rally, attracts hordes of riders to the Lake George area in early June.

Even off-season, you can enjoy a nice run up to Lake George via dependable Route 9. The road sweeps through slow curves and a few forgettable towns, campgrounds, and past random log cabins. The forest is tranquil and peaceful, and smooth back roads lead to the Adirondacks, Vermont, and Great Lake Sacandaga. Some say that I-87 North to Canada is one of the most scenic roads in the United States.

Lake George itself has a veneer as a tacky tourist town littered with T-shirt shops and mini-golf. Motels abound in Lake George and tourist cabins dot Route 9N. If you have time and a full tank, take a ride around Lake George—it's a magnificent lakeshore run.

Resources for Riders

Hudson River Valley Run

New York Travel Information

New York Camping Reservations—800/456-2267, www.reserveamerica.com
New York State Parks—www.nysparks.com
New York State Thruway Road Conditions—800/847-8929 or www.nysthruway.gov
New York State Travel and Tourism—800/225-5697, www.iloveny.com

Local and Regional Information

Adirondack Bed & Breakfast Association—www.adirondackbb.com
Dutchess County Tourism—845/463-4000 or 800/445-3131, www.dutchesstourism.com
Hudson River Valley Information—800/232-4782, www.hudsonvalley.org
Hyde Park Chamber of Commerce—845/229-8612, www.hydeparkchamber.org
Saratoga County Chamber of Commerce—518/584-3255 or 800/526-8970, www.saratoga.org
Sleepy Hollow Tarrytown Chamber of Commerce—914/631-1705, www.sleepyhollowchamber.com

New York Motorcycle Shops

Albany Honda—390 New Karner Rd., Albany, 518/452-1003
Brunswick Harley-Davidson/Buell—68 Weibel Ave., Saratoga Springs, 518/279-1145, www.brunswickharley.com
Dutchess Recreational Vehicles—737 Freedom Plains Rd. Poughkeepsie, 845/454-2810, www.dutchessrec.com
Ed's Service Motorcycles—600 Violet Ave., Hyde Park, 845/454-6210, www.eds-service.com
Haverstraw Motorsports—64–66 Rte. 9W, Haverstraw, 845/429-0141, www.haverstrawmotorsports.com
Prestige Harley-Davidson—205 Rte. 9W, Congers, 845/268-6651 or 866/668-7292, www.prestigeharleydavidson.com
Rockwell Cycles—1005 Rte. 9W, Fort Montgomery, 845/446-3834, www.rockwellcycles.com
Spitzies Harley-Davidson—1970 Central Ave., Albany, 518/456-7433 or 888/210-8481, www.spitzies.com
Woodstock Harley-Davidson—949 Rte. 28, Kingston, 845/338-2800, www.woodstockharley.com
Zack's V-Twin Cycles—799 Violet Ave., Hyde Park, 845/229-1177, www.zacksvtwin.com

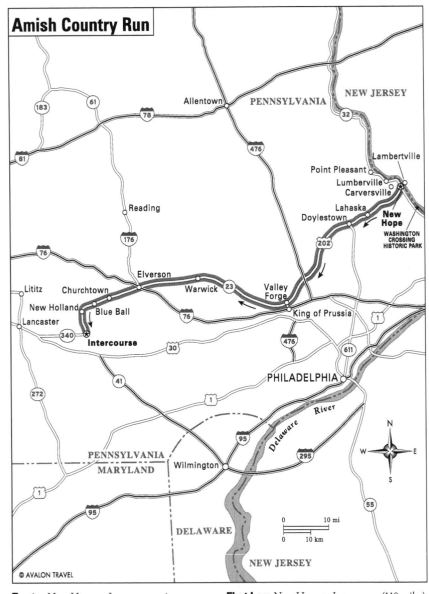

Amish Country Run

PENNSYLVANIA   **NEW JERSEY**

Allentown

183   61   78   476   32

81   Lambertville

Point Pleasant   Lumberville   Carversville

Reading   Lahaska   Doylestown   **New Hope**

176   202   **WASHINGTON CROSSING HISTORIC PARK**

76   Elverson

Lititz   Churchtown   Warwick   23   Valley Forge

New Holland   Blue Ball   76   King of Prussia   1

Lancaster   340   **Intercourse**   30   476   611

41   **PHILADELPHIA**

272   1   1   *Delaware River*

PENNSYLVANIA   95

MARYLAND   Wilmington   295

1   N W E S

95   0   10 mi   0   10 km   55

DELAWARE

© AVALON TRAVEL   **NEW JERSEY**

Route: New Hope to Intercourse via Lahaska, Doylestown, Valley Forge

Distance: Approximately 110 miles

First Leg: New Hope to Intercourse (110 miles)

Helmet Laws: Pennsylvania does not require helmets (conditions apply).

Amish Country Run
New Hope, Pennsylvania to Intercourse, Pennsylvania

This is a journey that will take you into the past, from the colonial accents an hour north of Philadelphia to a Revolutionary War landmark and then into the heart of 19th-century farmland. Along the way, you'll ride beside the historic Delaware River and also be presented with unlimited views of Pennsylvania's most pristine farmland. Some of America's finest back roads and friendliest people are found in this region.

NEW HOPE PRIMER

Few towns, I think, are so at ease with themselves as is New Hope. It seems to saunter through history content to take on whatever the era expects.

Of course it's had plenty of practice.

From its roots in the American Revolution, it reached new peaks in the 1930s when some of the nation's best playwrights introduced shows here. By the 1980s it had evolved into a yuppie-friendly village and since has continued to change with subtle shifts. When you arrive you'll probably view New Hope through the prism of your age. Young riders may see it as a nouveau/retro Haight-Ashbury; couples may see it as a place to bring the kids; and older motorcycle travelers will find a charming shopping village.

New Hope is all of this, but it is also something greater. It is a historic community that predates Philadelphia. It was at Coryell's Ferry where George Washington prepared for his fabled crossing of the river before making the real voyage a few miles south. A century later, the town became the birthplace of the New Hope School of Artists, whose members left Philadelphia to gain inspiration from the summer countryside and later fostered the Pennsylvania impressionist movement. It is an actors' community—as a young man, Robert Redford honed his skills here at the Bucks County Playhouse. It is a walking town where a short bridge spans the adjacent Delaware River and heads straight into downtown Lambertville, New Jersey.

Perfectly positioned about an hour south

of New York City and about an hour north of Philadelphia, New Hope is most of all a popular Point B for motorcycle travelers enjoying weekend runs from across New York, New Jersey, and Pennsylvania.

ON THE ROAD: NEW HOPE

You'll be floored by what you'll discover beyond the boundaries of New Hope; but before you head out, take some time and hang around town. If you've been here before, you'll notice that the once-exclusive veneer which had been created by New Hope's high-class galleries, cafés, and upscale boutiques has now given way to a more middle-class collection of independent cigar shops, bars, and variety shops that sell an abundance of quirky collectibles.

To find your feet, drop by the **visitors center** (1 W. Mechanic St., 215/862-5030), where you'll find maps, brochures, and guides that will introduce you to an impressive number of nearby attractions and sites. After taking a good look at the village—which is easily worth the investment of a half day or more—dodge the tourists and take off on Route 32 North (aka River Rd.) for a short, slow, and seductive ride beside the beautiful Delaware River.

Within a few miles, the trimmed hedges and manicured lawns of the town give way to some sharp curves, narrow roads, and a tunnel of green. Fresh fields and fat stone walls rise and fall with the earth as the road follows the lead of those walls, pushing you up and around tight corners and then face to face with a flood of spectacular scenery.

Since it's so easy to get into the groove of the road, it's hard to believe that this landscape is only a few miles from the downtown tourist scene. By the time you reach the junction of Routes 32 and 263 a

few miles later, you're well into the country and within view of **Dilly's Corner** (Rtes. 32 and 263, 215/862-5333, open seasonally Tues.–Sun.), a nostalgic diner where it seems everyone in Pennsylvania converges to load up on hamburgers, cheeseburgers, shakes, and sundaes.

Back on Route 32 North, you'll approach Lumberville and a wonderful stretch of woods that soon opens up to reveal the wide Delaware River on your right. Depending on the season, you may encounter a flotilla of people drifting lazily downriver in slick black innertubes.

This is a peaceful ride, and when you pass sections where landscaped lawns and untouched grasses grow side by side, there's a real satisfaction knowing that no one's screwed this up yet. Keep your eyes open because, coming up on your left in Lumberville, the Old Carversville Road rises steeply. When you get on this hard-packed back road, it puts you in the thick of the woods, where small cabins and homes are hidden well below a thicket of tall trees and snaking limbs. The road is narrow and the woods are quiet and, after several miles, you'll reach one small bridge and then another and then you arrive in the heart of Carversville.

Compared to the solitude of the forest road, it seems like there's a lot of action here even though downtown's only about the size of an average backyard. Aside from the landmark inn across the street, most activity is taking place at the **Carversville General Store** (215/297-5353). Well-stocked with groceries, drinks, and a small diner, it does double duty as the town post office and theater. How so? On the last Monday of each summer month, they project them "moving picture shows" onto the side of the building.

After retracing your route back through the forest road toward Lumberville, turn

Not all soldiers made it across the Delaware on Christmas night, 1776. Some young patriots ended up here—in a cemetery upriver of Washington Crossing.

left to follow Route 32 North again. When you pass the village of Devil's Half Acre, the stunning views and weaving road unleash you into some Le Mans–style driving that'll sweep you into small bumps and quick ascents. The best part of the ride is finding that along this one road in the Delaware Valley, there's very little commercialism, so for now it's just the road and you.

Several miles on is Point Pleasant, home of **Bucks County River Country** (215/297-5000, www.rivercountry.net), the point of origin for the armada of inner tube passengers you passed downriver. For me, places like this make a tour great. There's a village store here and if you have time and a bathing suit, rent a tube, raft, canoe, or kayak and take the day off; just cruise down the Delaware, drifting at a lazy 1.5 mph in cool water. There are no rapids, so just relax and enjoy the soothing, peaceful experience.

From here, you can continue your northward trek toward Upper Black Eddy and Lake Nockamixon, or dash east along the Delaware into Frenchtown, New Jersey, or take virtually any road in any direction for a longer ride, or turn back and head home to New Hope.

That's the beauty of New Hope and its surroundings. No matter where you ride, you'll be satisfied.

PULL IT OVER: NEW HOPE HIGHLIGHTS
Attractions and Adventures

Seven remarkably cool, must-ride miles south of New Hope is the site of a turning point in American history: **Washington Crossing Historic Park** (1112 River Rd./Rte. 32, Washington Crossing, 215/493-4076, www.ushistory.org/washingtoncrossing). On a slushy and sleeting Christmas 1776, George Washington massed part of the Continental Army and took a gamble on the future of America—which turned out to be a much bigger

The Crux of the Crossing

There's a strong chance that America wouldn't exist today had it not been for the actions of Washington and his men on Christmas 1776. No one knew if they would make it. Knowing that his men needed inspiration, a few days before their mission to cross the Delaware and attack the Hessians, Washington had Thomas Paine's *The American Crisis* read aloud to his troops. Did it help? Consider this opening paragraph and then consider how you would have felt.

These are the times that try men's souls: The summer soldier and the sunshine patriot will, in this crisis, shrink from the service of their country; but he that stands it now, deserves the love and thanks of man and woman. Tyranny, like hell, is not easily conquered; yet we have this consolation with us, that the harder the conflict, the more glorious the triumph. What we obtain too cheap, we esteem too lightly: it is dearness only that gives every thing its value.

gamble than he expected. Of the three divisions scheduled to cross the river that night, only Washington and his men managed the nearly impossible feat. What's more, they marched nearly ten miles, many barefoot, through the snow to reach Trenton in time to attack and defeat 900 Hessian mercenaries and capture enough food and supplies to sustain themselves through the brutal winter of 1777.

If you only know Washington from the dollar bill, get to know the real man by watching the introductory video and visiting the historic buildings and boathouse stacked with replicas of the workhouse Durham boats. Here's another tip: On the return trip to New Hope, stop and pay your respects to his spirit and those of the young soldiers buried near the river at a Revolutionary War cemetery a few miles on. It's about halfway between Washington Crossing and New Hope on Route 32 (about five miles northwest of the park's visitors center).

The phrase "iron horse" originally referred to locomotives but, over generations, was attached to motorcycles. You can experience the original incarnation at the **New Hope & Ivyland Railroad** (32 W. Bridge St., 215/862-2332, www.newhope-erailroad.com, from $17). They have four steam locomotives and Number 40 is a 1925 full-gauge model that pulls passenger cars through the hills and valleys of Bucks County. If that gets your motor going, give serious thought to upgrading to the rare "locomotive cab ride," since this is one of few steam railroads that allows passengers to ride up front with the engineers. Trips depart several times daily in season.

Perhaps the most casual cruising experience anywhere would be with the **New Hope Canal Boat Company** (149 S. Main St., 215/862-0758, www.canalboats.com, about $10). The Delaware Canal flows sixty miles between Easton and Bristol, and from New Hope a mule team will pull your barge along for several miles along the canal to show you a different side of New Hope. If you're traveling in a group, call ahead to reserve a private barge for a canal party—and stock up on a cooler full of beer.

© NANCY HOWELL

Visit Washington Crossing and your image of Washington will change from an old man on a dollar bill to a man of mythic heroism.

Right in the heart of town, **Bucks County Playhouse** (70 South Main St., 215/862-2041 or 215/862-2046, www.buckscountyplayhouse.com), is the state theater of Pennsylvania. Far enough from Broadway to try out plays and close enough to take them to NYC if they were any good, this has been a launching pad for great playwrights like George S. Kaufman and Moss Hart. Hopeful actors Robert Redford, Grace Kelly, Dick Van Dyke, Tyne Daly, and Liza Minnelli caught the stage right here. Tickets for main stage shows are around $25.

In addition to floating down the Delaware in an inner tube, you can head to **Coryell's Ferry** (22 S. Main St., 215/862-2050) for a 45-minute cruise on the river, picking up intelligence about the history of the area and what happened the night Washington made his crossing. It's still in the same location where John Wells— the town's founder and first ferryboat

operator—began his business in 1718 and where, in 1776, patriot John Coryell provided service to Washington's troops and to America by keeping the Redcoats stranded on the opposite bank.

Shopping

There are several stores in the heart of town that feature leather in various configurations. The one you really want to see was created by Joe "NY Joe" Wynne, a motorcycle enthusiast and former co-manager of NYC H-D. **After the Ride** (115 S. Main St., 609/862-0172, www.aftertheride.com) features moto-clothing, jewelry, and high-end leathers, some of it even custom tailored. Who wears their hypercool "pyrate" fashions? Keith Richards, Ozzy Osborne, Laurence Fishburne, Will Smith, and Aerosmith, for starts. **Fred Eisen Leather Design** (129 S. Main St, 215/862-5988, www.fredeisenleather.com) sells Indian-style clothing, as well as belts and saddlebags with a Western theme. A few doors down, **Sterling Leather** (97 S. Main St., 215/862-9669, www.sterlingleather.com) sells a similar line of hats, moccasins, boots, and accessories. At **Living Arts Tattoo** (12 W. Mechanic St., 215/862-3816) you can pick up an indelible souvenir, from a tiny first tattoo to an elaborate custom piece.

Aging baby boomers trying to retrieve the junk they threw away can buy it back at **Love Saves the Day** (1 S. Main St., 215/862-1399), which is crammed with Beatles memorabilia, lunch boxes, '60s TV merchandise, old Playboys, vintage clothing, black velvet Springsteen, and rare Star Wars items which, I guess, are all a far site more valuable than the contents of a Bernie Madoff portfolio.

If you'd like to stash a few books in your saddlebags, head to **Farley's Bookshop** (44 S. Main St., 215/862-2452, farleysbookshop.com) and load up on literature. The store is filled with rooms stacked with shelves loaded with an uncommonly huge amount of new books and magazines.

Across the river at the former OTC Cracker Factory, **River Horse Brewing** (80 Lambert Ln., Lambertville, 609/397-7776, www.riverhorse.com) brews a half-dozen kinds of beer at any one time. Order 'em all and enjoy a six-pack. It's open noon–5 P.M., so you can walk through the brewery, buy gifts in the store, and get samples in the sampling room.

Blue-Plate Specials

Over the Delaware River at **Sneddon's Luncheonette** (47 Bridge St., 609/397-3053, Lambertville), the sound of dishes slapping and silverware clanging go right along with the old-fashioned wood paneling and heart-shaped wireback chairs. The home-cooked breakfasts and lunches, mostly soups and sandwiches, will take you back home (provided your home was a diner).

There are numerous fine dining restaurants around New Hope, but one of my favorites is **Wildflowers Garden Restaurant** (8 W. Mechanic St., 215/862-2241, www.wildflowersnewhope.com). It stands out for having good food that doesn't cost a fortune (around $10 for lunch and $15 for dinner). Although the outdoor patio may be crowded, the riverside setting is the perfect place to relax and experience New Hope. Entrees feature such diverse fare as Yankee pot roast and extremely tasty Thai food. I highly recommend it.

Watering Holes

Evenings are as enjoyable as days in New Hope, and being in a walking town means you can park your bike and bar-hop your way across the river into New Jersey. Start in New Hope at the crowded and cool **Fran's Pub** (116 S. Main St., 215/862-5539), which entertains with a pool table, jukebox, pizzas, burgers, sandwiches, widescreen TV, and a cooler filled with beers. Look around and notice that tattoos are as abundant as brands of brew. Enjoy happy hour (4:30–6:30 P.M.) on the nice outdoor patio, a great place for people-watching.

Every night at **John and Peter's** (96 S. Main St., 215/862-5981, www.johnandpeters.com) is like a talent show audition. Since 1972, folks have packed this low-key joint to be treated to shows by such performers as Leon Redbone, George Thorogood, Norah Jones, and Martin Mull—and nearly 50,000 other acts. It's got a neat patio and a cool atmosphere and if it's Monday and you're talented, drunk, or both, take part in open mic night. Smoking is allowed.

Up and down Main Street, you'll find other sidewalk cafés, open-air bars, and places heralded as "martini bars" and "libation lounges." One noteworthy spot is **Havana's** (105 S. Main St., 215/862-9897, www.havananewhope.com). On a typical night, it's packed with revelers enjoying the expansive, laid-back, Key West patio–style setting and full liquor bar. Here since 1978, Havana's has the good sense to feature blues, rockabilly, R&B, and funk acts.

Shut-Eye

With its only motel going out of business, and large chain hotels changing names, the best chance to find a room is in a bed-and-breakfast. They are plentiful in New Hope and in neighboring communities like Lambertville and Lumberville. The good news is that competition between the inns raised the level of service and comfort; the not-so-good news is that prices rose as well. There are far too many to list, so for a complete and current listing check www.newhopechamber.com (215/862-9990) and follow the link to Lodging.

Inn-dependence

A small property in a nice setting, **Porches** (20 Fishers Alley, 215/862-3277, www.porchesnewhope.com, $95 and up weekdays) is an 1880s cottage-style home in the heart of town, with the nicer and more private rooms in annex buildings on the property. The pace is informal, and most of the 1920s-decor rooms overlook the Delaware Canal Towpath. After a full country breakfast of fruit, bacon, sausage, pancakes, and fresh bread, you can waddle off to start your day.

Also in town are two notable historic inns: **Wedgwood Inn** and its sibling **Aaron Burr House Inn** (80 and 111 W. Bridge St., 215/862-2570, www.wedgwoodinn.com and www.aaronburrhouse.com, $95–125). Both are traditional with 20 individually decorated rooms to choose from, some with tubs, fireplaces, king beds, and bay windows. The screened flagstone patio is a relaxing setting. In addition to a full breakfast, owner Carl serves complimentary hot and cold drinks and other refreshments in the afternoon, and in the evening chocolates and a nip of his secret-recipe almond liqueur.

The setting for the **1740 House** (3690 River Rd., Lumberville, 215/297-5661, www.1740house.com, $150 and up) is perfect, albeit pricey for a moto-tour. It's a little way out of town; the advantage is being on a beautiful site overlooking the Delaware and having a riverside pool to relax in when you've finished your ride. Each of the 23 rooms is decorated in Early American style, and each has a balcony and a river view.

Chain Drive

These chain hotels are in town, or within 10 miles of the city center:

Courtyard by Marriott, Hampton Inn
For more information, including phone numbers and websites, see page 99.

ON THE ROAD: NEW HOPE TO INTERCOURSE

If I were in an episode of *The Twilight Zone*—the kind where somebody's stuck someplace forever—I would hope Rod Serling would send me riding endlessly across the Pennsylvania countryside. This desire starts in the rides around New Hope and continues upon leaving New Hope on Route 202 towards Lahaska. On the way out of town, you'll pass a complex called **Peddler's Village** (215/794-4000, www.peddlersvillage.com) and while it looks like a tourist trap, the 70 stores and nearly a dozen restaurants that spread across a shopping village are not too bad. Plus, it's not so far from New Hope that you couldn't frequent one of their pubs and

The spirit of George Washington and the determination of his men are celebrated in the magnificent Washington Arch of Valley Forge.

© NANCY HOWELL

taverns and, provided you're sober, ride back to town.

Stay on Route 202 and you'll ride into Doylestown, a picture-perfect town that's small enough for a manageable and brief stop. Downtown is particularly clean and nice, with a movie theater, bookstore, and various independent merchants. One of the prime attractions here is the interesting **James A. Michener Art Museum** (138 S. Pine St., 215/340-9800, www.michenermuseum.com), named for Doylestown native, famed author, and philanthropist James Michener. Located in a refurbished 1880s prison, it showcases rotating exhibits as well as Michener and his works, and other Bucks County residents including Pearl S. Buck, Oscar Hammerstein II, Moss Hart, George S. Kaufman, Dorothy Parker, and S. J. Perelman.

When you follow Route 202 out of Doylestown, you'll be riding toward King of Prussia and I'm afraid the road will fizzle out for a long stretch. A less taxing alternative is riding in an arc well north of King of Prussia to explore roads that link small towns like Lansdale, North Wales, Gwynedd, and Skippack. There are too many turns to list here, but eventually, you'll take Valley Forge Road to descend toward the front door of this spectacular historical gem.

Though never the site of a battle, as in Washington Crossing this is where America's pursuit of liberty hung in the balance. By surviving the harsh winter of 1777–1778 and the loss of 2,000 men to the elements, Washington's troops proved they were tough enough to see the Revolution through to its conclusion. That's why you should stop at the **Valley Forge National Historical Park** (610/783-1077, www.nps. gov/vafo). You probably won't visit in winter, but you may still feel chills when you think about what happened in this place.

Take off on a superb 10-mile loop tour around the 3,500-acre site, knowing that when morale dropped, Washington offered $12 to the soldiers who constructed the first log cabin built to his specs. It worked. The men created new shelters and, with the arrival of a Prussian officer named Friedrich Wilhelm Ludolf Gerhard Augustin von Steuben (aka Baron von Steuben), they also developed a new sense of discipline and esprit de corps. Along the ride are replicas of these cabins as well as monuments that dot the roadside. It doesn't cost anything to see the museum and film at the visitors center, and in May 2009 they re-opened the home that served as headquarters for Washington and his staff (making it the Pentagon of its day). Take advantage of the museum and historical movies, and pay tribute to the people who endured the winter to help create a nation.

Within miles, as you begin the ride west from Valley Forge, you'll see that the road gets significantly and magnificently nicer as Route 23 forms a slow arc through the low hills. The road is absolutely perfect with scenery that is vibrant and energizing, cool and warm. In regions like the French Creek Watershed District, there are a series of nice hills and dips with expansive farmlands spreading off to the horizons north and south. Over and over again come wonderful small towns like Warwick, Elverson, Churchtown, and Blue Ball, where the extraordinarily fertile orchards, groves, and fields are visible reminders of why you ride. Your own free-riding spirit is matched by that of home-crafters who have posted signs to sell handmade cedar chests, quilts, and root beer.

In the town of New Holland, New Holland Road leads to the south en route to Route 340. You know you're entering the heart of Amish Country because the sweet smell of fields of produce gives way to the odiferous aroma of Amish farms and horse-drawn buggies. But the scents are worth the price of admission because they signify that, once you turn west on Route 340, you'll soon be enjoying Intercourse.

INTERCOURSE PRIMER

It was one of the most amazing sights of my journey. As I rode into Intercourse and raised my visor, the blunt chill of the evening air hit my face. I scanned the road, and a motion drew my attention to the ridge of a hill. An Amish farmer stood tall on the back of a mule-driven wagon and the hay was stacked high behind him. Silhouetted against the setting sun, he was a vision from 1820. I was in Intercourse and in the past.

This place was originally called Cross Key, but the name was changed because of (select one): A) the intersecting roads, B) the entrance to a horse racing track, or C) the "intercourse," or social interaction

and support that's symbolic of the village. The residents can't agree either. Although Lancaster gets the tourists, Intercourse is the hub of the Amish people. Surrounded by farmlands, Intercourse is a museum without walls—although the walls are closing in. A few miles in any direction are modern buildings and businesses that must surely tempt young farmers.

While New Hope's Bucks County thrives on culture and diversity, the strengths of Lancaster County are dining and simplicity. There's not much shakin' at night; but during the day, there are fantastic country roads to ride and the most satisfying roadside restaurants you'll ever find.

ON THE ROAD: INTERCOURSE

When you hit the road in Intercourse don't expect to be treated like Harrison Ford in *Witness*. No, the Amish aren't going to ask you to strap on a tool belt and help raise a barn and they probably won't welcome

© NANCY HOWELL

No tractors or combines in Amish Country. Just manual labor and pristine farmland.

The Amish Way of Life

No stress, no worries. The joy of being a kid is evident on the faces of Amish children gathered at a local pond.

Despite their identification as the Pennsylvania Dutch, Amish ancestors hailed from Germany, not Holland. They left Deutschland (get it?) to seek religious freedom. Today's Lancaster County "Old Order Amish" stress humility, family, community, and separation from the world. All Old Order members drive buggies, not cars. Their homes do not have electricity, and their children are educated as far as the eighth grade in one-room schoolhouses.

As for personal appearance, Amish women seldom cut their hair, and they wear a black prayer covering if they're single and a white one if they're married. Men wear dark suits, straight-cut coats with lapels, suspenders, solid-colored shirts, and black or straw broad-brimmed hats. It's not a costume, but an expression of their faith. It's also worth noting that they don't avoid change entirely. They just take longer to consider a new product before deciding to accept or reject it. So, don't discount an Amish data encryption service.

I spoke with a Mennonite resident of Intercourse who explained the Amish policy of giving young men free rein to leave the church and community, known as "rumspringa." He told me, "It's like this way: You're getting taught from a young age what's right and what's wrong. So, when you're 18, you're an adult and you're supposed to know what's right and what's wrong, and then when you learn temptations, you're on your own. If you do wrong, then you're dealing with the law."

But Amish youth must deal with more than mere legal pressures. If an Amish youth forsakes his lessons and upbringing, giving in to the same temptations as his "English" peers, he's considered an outcast from the church and the community and cannot return.

you into their homes, either. But if you're respectful and keep your camera out of sight, you won't be viewed as one of the rude "English" either.

Aside from hanging around the general stores in town, maybe the best way to understand and appreciate the community is to pick up one of the widely distributed maps of Amish Country. Quite detailed and easy to follow, it reveals dozens of roads that intersect the farms here and as long as you remain within the rough rectangle they form, you can ride for many miles and many hours without seeing a trace of progress.

One route leaves Intercourse on Route 340 East, passing Spring Garden and White Horse and turning left onto Churchtown Road before Compass. So far, the ride reveals nothing out of the ordinary, but when you turn left (north), you'll notice there are no phone or electrical lines running to the homes. Their absence makes the landscape as pure and authentic as any place you'll find.

Follow the road all the way to Route 23, then turn left to head west. You're on the periphery of the Amish farms, returning past small towns like New Holland and Bareville. Near Leola, turn left (south) on Route 772 and the road will put you in the thick of the farms. The ride is quiet and calm, interrupted occasionally by a horse-drawn carriage or hay wagon rolling down the lane. You won't tire of the sight, but be very careful riding at night, since these dark carriages can be hard to see.

Speaking of night riding, you may want to try it at least once. I did, and what I took to be a massive region of nothing turned out to be a busy farming area—but I couldn't tell until I saw that I was riding just yards away from massive farmhouses. Nearly hidden in the dark, they were lit only by candles and lanterns.

Sharp 90-degree curves dividing the farms keep you alert, as will the crop of Amish children who gather near the road to stare at you and your bike when you ride past. Route 772 takes a sharp right at Hess Road, where you turn and continue on Route 772 to a scenic road called Scenic Road (really). Now do yourself a favor and get lost. With U.S. 30 to the south and Route 23 to the north, you may pass the Amish equivalent of a commercial district: buggies lined up at repair shops, tobacco drying in barns, and carpenters crafting simple furniture with even simpler tools.

While any day's great for a ride here, head out on a Sunday morning and you'll see hundreds of Amish worshippers walking and rolling down country roads to church, a service that's usually held in the home of a fellow parishioner. It's an unusual sight because, of nearly any other place in America, these may be the most "country" country roads you can ride. Each road will tempt you, and if you want to go off on a tear, have at it. Get lost. Explore. And enjoy your ride into the past.

PULL IT OVER: INTERCOURSE HIGHLIGHTS
Attractions and Adventures

There's really not a lot going on in Intercourse, so you may as well not do anything at the **Kitchen Kettle Village** (Rte. 340, 717/768-8261 or 800/732-3538, www.kitchenkettle.com). Actually, this is a popular little shopping village so there's a chance you may find a new pair of handcrafted leather boots, score some fresh-off-the-lathe furniture, or listen to some folk musicians. If your bike is wired for sound, this is where you can pick up an in-depth audio tour of Amish country. The village is open 9 A.M.–5 P.M. daily.

It's an expensive diversion (prices float close to $200), but the **United States Hot**

Air Balloon Team (141 Hopewell Rd., Elverson, 610/469-0782 or 800/763-5987, www.ushotairballoon.com) takes daily flights over the Amish farmland. Be sure before you commit—baskets can hold up to eight people so your vision of a private excursion is possible, but not likely. They have two launch sites, one in St. Peters and one in Lancaster. You can help prepare the balloon for flight, and then settle in for a long drift over the rolling country-side, followed by snacks and a champagne toast. You'll have to leave your bike on the ground.

Compared to Intercourse, Lancaster's a metropolis (which is why I steer clear), but there's something worth seeing here on Tuesday, Friday, and Saturday mornings. The historic **Central Market** (717/291-4723), in the heart of Lancaster at Penn Square, has been at this location since the 1730s and is America's oldest publicly owned, continuously operated farmers market. It may take a few hours to figure out how to strap a dozen bags of farm-fresh produce, pastries, syrups, salmon cakes, quarts of milk, flowers, crab cakes, baked goods, chow-chows, and relishes onto your bike, but it'll be worth it. Back toward town on pleasing Route 340, the **Bird in Hand Farmers Market** (2710 Old Philadelphia Pike/Rte. 340, 717/393-9674, www.birdinhandfarmersmarket.com) is smaller but equally popular. A load of Amish farmers sell here as well, and when you look into their doleful eyes, I doubt you can escape without buying some homemade products, whether it's pickles, fudge, nuts, jellies, or jellied pickle nut fudge. Really, really good stuff.

In the heart of Intercourse, **W. L. Zimmerman and Sons** (3601 Old Philadelphia Pike/Rte. 340, 717/768-8291) is where the Amish and English shop for dry goods and groceries. Opened in 1909, the store caters to its base by offering an amazing inventory of products last seen in a 1939 A&P catalogue. Although a larger store has opened next door, in this old store you'll be shopping shoulder to shoulder with taciturn young Amish men and their equally stoic wives.

Blue-Plate Specials

Although Amish country is shy on tattoo parlors and tanning salons, there's no shortage of great restaurants, the kind you crave when you're on the road or have just raised a barn. In some cases, you'll share a large table with other travelers.

Slightly smaller than Beijing, the **Plain & Fancy Farm** (3121 Old Philadelphia Pike/Rte. 340, Bird-in-Hand, 717/768-4400, www.plainandfancyfarm.com) serves food nearly as large. This ranks among my five favorite road food pit stops, and the busloads of diners here would concur. Lunch and dinner are served at huge picnic tables inside the barnlike building, where you'll eat as much roast beef, sausage, chicken, mashed potatoes, bow-tie noodles, vegetables, and ice cream as your big ol' belly can hold. And how many places do you know serve shoofly pie?

The Smucker family does well producing filling country foods, the kind you'll find at **Bird-in-Hand Family Restaurant** (2760 Old Philadelphia Pike/Rte. 340, Bird-in-Hand, 717/768-1550, www.bird-in-hand.com). The menu features ham, pork and sauerkraut, lima beans, roast turkey, new potatoes, and the like. Most items are made from scratch (such as the home-made soups), with some ingredients and dishes delivered by Amish farmers. And aside from Plain & Fancy Farm, how many places do you know serve shoofly pie?

Stoltzfus Farm Restaurant (Rte. 772 E., 717/768-8156, www.stoltzfusfarm-restaurant.com), serves big food, such as homemade sausage, chicken, hamloaf, chow-chow, applesauce, apple butter, sweet potatoes, and corn, plus desserts like cherry crumb, apple crumb, and fresh shoofly pie. And how many places do you know serve shoofly pie? Yes, three is the correct answer. Open for lunch and dinner daily except Sunday, closed December–March.

In a little truck stop in 1929, Anna Miller cooked up chicken and waffles for travelers. Today, **Miller's Smorgasbord** (Rte. 30 one mile east of Rte. 896, 717/687-6621) serves lunch and dinner daily, plus breakfast every day in season. Mix and match omelettes, pancakes, French toast, homemade breads, soups, baked apples, roast turkey, baked ham, fried chicken, fish, shrimp, sautéed mushrooms, mashed potatoes, baked cabbage, chicken pot pie, cakes, and pies that'll kick off your very own sumo wrestler training program.

Shut-Eye

Thanks to its relative closeness to Lancaster, there are countless lodging choices. But ask anyone, and they'll tell you it's better in Intercourse.

Inn-dependence

I would rank the **Amish Country Inns & Spa** (3542 Old Philadelphia Pike, 717/768-2626 or 800/664-0949, www.amishcountryinns.com, $149 and up) as one of America's best inns. Elmer Thomas restored this 1909 Victorian home, and his staff practices courtesy as art. The rooms befit a five-star hotel, the breakfasts are superb, and the top-floor suite is great for couples. Rates start at $149 and reach as high as (yipes!) $379 for the largest suite. Out back, Elmer created themed cottages, which feature large rooms, microwaves, desks, fireplaces, generous baths, whirlpool tubs, fridges, wet bars, and Amish furnishings built specially for the rooms. Suffice it to say this is absolutely first-rate for riders who can splurge. Elmer's son runs the other recommended option in the heart of town: the **Best Western Intercourse Village Inn** (Rtes. 340 and 772, 717/768-3636 or 800/717-6202, $109–139). A standard hotel, it nonetheless stays true to Elmer's vision of cleanliness and friendliness. An on-site restaurant serves home-cooked breakfast, lunch, and dinner. There are laundry facilities here, too.

Chain Drive

These chain hotels are in town, or within 10 miles of the city center: **Best Western, Comfort Inn, Days Inn, Econo Lodge, Fairfield Inn, Hampton Inn, Holiday Inn, Howard Johnson, Knights Inn, Motel 6, Quality Inn, Ramada, Red Carpet Inn, Rodeway, Scottish Inns, Sleep Inn, Super 8, Travelodge**

Fill 'er up! A barn-size ad for dairy fresh milk in Amish Country.

© NANCY HOWELL

For more information, including phone numbers and websites, see page 99.

SIDE TRIP: LITITZ

One of the peak moments in motorcycle touring is when you discover a new town that hasn't been harmed by homogenization. From the northwest corner of the previous ride (on Route 772), it's only a short ride to Lititz (north of Lancaster) where almost nothing has happened and which sports that look favored by Norman Rockwell. Ride Route 772 north into this small town, and you'll arrive in a busy little shopping district with a Main Street and a shaded park centered around a stream and natural spring and all of the essentials to qualify as a neat town. There's the historic **General Sutter Inn** (14 E. Main St., 717/626-2115, www.generalsutterinn.com, $70–130), which features the 1764 Restaurant and 16 spacious rooms. It's tempting to stay the night. Around the corner, **Glassmyer's Restaurant** (23 N. Broad St., 717/626-2345), serves diner meals topped off by creations like egg creams and phosphates from the old-fashioned soda fountain.

But the highlight of Lititz is the aphrodisiacal aroma wafting from the **Wilbur Chocolate Factory** (48 N. Broad St., 717/626-3249, www.wilburbuds.com). Chances are you've never heard of or received a box of Wilbur Chocolates, but that shouldn't stop you from sniffing your way around the Candy Americana Museum, which details the history of cocoa, the life cycle of a candy bar, and Wilbur's "Wheel of Fortune" candy horoscope. A gift shop features T-shirts, ordinary candy, and a gift pack containing five 10-pound chocolate bars—yes, *50 pounds* of chocolate bargain-priced at $179. Overhead, the ceiling rumbles beneath the weight of Wilbur gears and belts cranking out another batch of chocolates.

Provided you don't fall into a diabetic coma, spend some time bumming around downtown and then take your time riding back on the country roads of your choice. On the boomerang return, you'll pass Mennonite children skimming through the hills on simple scooters, farmers selling fresh produce, flowers, homemade bread, and root beer. You may even pass the random harness maker who can turn his expertise at creating harnesses into making custom saddlebags for your own iron horse.

Resources for Riders

Amish Country Run

Pennsylvania Travel Information

Pennsylvania Road Conditions—866/976-8747, www.paturnpike.com
Pennsylvania State Parks—888/727-2757, www.dcnr.state.pa.us
Pennsylvania Tourism and Lodging Information—717/232-8880, www.patourism.org
Pennsylvania Visitor Information—800/847-4872, www.visitpa.com

Local and Regional Information

Bucks County Visitors Bureau—215/639-0300 or 800/836-2825, www.bccvb.org
Harrisburg (Intercourse) Weather—814/231-2408
Lambertville (NJ) Chamber of Commerce—609/397-0055, www.lambertville.org
Lancaster County (Intercourse) Information—717/299-8901 or 800/723-8824, www.padutchcountry.com
New Hope Chamber of Commerce—215/862-9990, www.newhope-pa.com
New Hope Visitors Center—215/862-5030, www.newhopevisitorscenter.org

Pennsylvania Motorcycle Shops

Action Motorsports—1881 Whiteford Rd., York, 717/757-2688, www.actionmotorsportsyork.com
B&B Yamaha—343 Champ Blvd., Mannheim, 717/898-5764, www.bblancasterpa.com
Classic Harley-Davidson—983 James Dr., Leesport, 610/916-7777, www.classicharley.com
Don's Kawasaki—20 E. Market St., Hallam (York), 717/755-6002, www.donskawasaki.com
Lancaster Harley-Davidson—308 Beaver Valley Pike, Willow Street, 717/464-2703, www.lancasterhd.com
Laugermans Harley-Davidson—100 Arsenal Rd., York, 717/854-3214, www.laugerman.com
Ray's Yamaha Polaris Victory—5560 Perkiomen, Reading, 610/582-2700, www.raysyamahapolarisvictory.com
Sport Cycle Suzuki—309 Hafer Dr., Leesport, 610/916-5000, www.sportcyclesuzuki.com

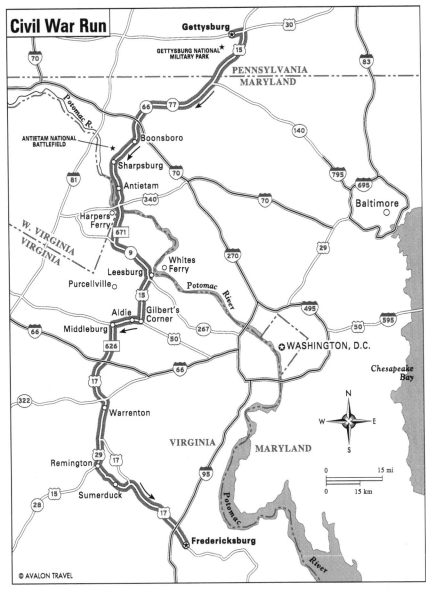

Route: Gettysburg to Fredericksburg via Catoctin Mountain Park, Antietam, Harpers Ferry, Leesburg

Distance: Approximately 170 miles

First Leg: Gettysburg, Pennsylvania to Leesburg, Viriginia (92 miles)

Second Leg: Leesburg to Fredericksburg, Virginia (80 miles)

Helmet Laws: Pennsylvania does not require helmets for riders over 21; Maryland, Virginia, and West Virginia require helmets.

Civil War Run
Gettysburg, Pennsylvania to Fredericksburg, Virginia

As you ease into this Pennsylvania ride, you may sense that the state is a microcosm of American history. From the Declaration of Independence to the Exposition of 1876, from Amish farmland to the fields of Gettysburg, it seems that everything we're about is all contained right here.

This will be a poignant trip through the killing fields of Pennsylvania, then across a mood-changing Maryland state park, past Civil War highlights, and into two historic Virginia walking towns. The route may not reveal all there is to know about the Civil War, but along the way you'll gain an appreciation for the countryside and your country.

GETTYSBURG PRIMER

In July 1863, Confederate soldiers were headed for Harrisburg, intent on capturing the city. But when an advance team ran across Union troops, the encounter sparked the flash point of the Battle of Gettysburg. Within three days, the Civil War reached its turning point as Robert E. Lee's 75,000 men and George G. Meade's 97,000 soldiers faced off. At the height of the battle, more than 172,000 men and 634 cannons were spread out over 25 square miles. When the final shot was fired, 51,000 casualties bloodied the fields.

Although the war continued for two more years, the Battle of Gettysburg broke the spirit and strength of the Confederacy. Months after the battle, the dedication of the Soldiers National Cemetery at Gettysburg gave President Lincoln the opportunity to praise the sacrifice of the soldiers and state what he felt were essential truths about our experiment with democracy.

To be sure, this has evolved into a tourist town with more than two million people arriving each year to tour the battlefields, and a million more arriving to see the town itself. While roughly a century and a half of progress has added modern touches to the town, the hallowed grounds of the battlefields have been well preserved to honor the sacrifices and bravery of men on both sides of the conflict.

ON THE ROAD: GETTYSBURG

Gettysburg's legend in American history is so large, it's surprising to find that the actual places of note are confined within a relatively small area. At its core Gettysburg is still a small town and as you walk through the historic district, try to picture it circa 1863 when only small farms were found in the outlying countryside. Use your imagination to visualize the community then and try to picture the people living in peace when all hell broke loose.

The town square is bisected by U.S. 15 Business Route, the main north–south road through town, and by east–west U.S. 30. This is the perfect base for your tour since you'll experience the richness of history both here and at the battlefield visitor center, about a mile south.

But first, bordering the town square are two sites worth a stop. On the southeast side of the square, the **David Wills House** (8 Lincoln Sq., 717/334-2599, www.davidwillshouse.org), is the home of the young lawyer who extended the invitation

Honest Abe gives an honest reaction to *Great American Motorcycle Tours:* He loves it.

to Lincoln to make "a few appropriate remarks." After arriving, Lincoln stayed in the second-floor room and worked on his speech the night before the dedication of the cemetery. Completely restored, for $6.50 you can visit the entire home as well as Lincoln's room and see related exhibits and mementoes. For an interesting photo, outside the home is a life-size statue of Lincoln talking to a statue that looks like Perry Como. Stand in front of Perry and pose with the president.

Across the street, the **Gettysburg Hotel** (1 Lincoln Sq., 717/337-2000, www.hotelgettysburg.com) has welcomed its share of presidents as well, primarily Eisenhower and his staff, who stayed here when the summer White House came to town.

After walking the square, ride south down U.S. 15 Business Route turning onto Route 97 to reach the new in 2008 $100 million battlefield visitor center. Obviously, you'll want to ride the battlefield, but do this only after taking a guided tour since it's important to know where you are to understand what you are seeing. After a tour you'll know more about places such as Little Round Top and the site of Pickett's Charge. From the summit of Little Round Top, you overlook the "Valley of Death" bordered by Devil's Den, a haven for Southern sharpshooters. Then there's one of the saddest places in America: the infamous "Wheatfield," where 6,000 Union and Confederate soldiers were killed, wounded, or captured during just four hours of bloody fighting.

After your guided tour, head to the **The Gettysburg National Military Park Visitor Center** (1195 Baltimore Pike, 717/334-1124, www.nps.gov/gett), where park rangers will fill in the blanks. They'll tell you about the 3,500 soldiers killed here and buried in the cemetery, nearly 1,000 of their identities known only to

© NANCY HOWELL

A monument of General Gouverneur K. Warren keeps watch over the Valley of Death at Little Round Top in Gettysburg.

God. You'll hear about the battle and its terrible aftermath—the burial of the dead, bodies being eaten by hogs, and looters whose punishment was burying dead horses. But what you'll want to hear most is the story of Lincoln's visit and the Gettysburg Address.

You may have read Lincoln's speech, but only after you've seen Gettysburg will you understand its importance. It was Lincoln's "I Have a Dream" speech as he re-affirmed the pursuit of democracy and, in less than two minutes and 300 words, addressed the nation's past, present, and future. After the speech was back in his pocket, "the United States are" became "the United States is" with Lincoln laying out how the war could save the nation envisioned by the authors of the Constitution.

From Little Round Top to the site of Pickett's Charge, this is a spiritual ride. Ride later in the day or very early in the morning when the tourist crowds thin.

That's when you can take your time to really see the roads and retrace the trails forged by soldiers of both sides, and you cannot help but be moved by the experience.

PULL IT OVER: GETTYSBURG HIGHLIGHTS
Attractions and Adventures

The **Gettysburg National Military Park Visitor Center** (1195 Baltimore Pike, 717/334-1124, www.nps.gov/gett) is ground zero for your Gettysburg experience. To see what needs to be seen in the cemetery, travel with a tour guide. Each day during the summer there are about 20 free ranger-led tours and, not surprisingly, the best and most enlightening information comes straight from these men and women whose love of history is palpable. A separate fee (about $10) will get you into the introductory film "A New Birth of Freedom," the cyclorama painting of the battle, and the museum which exhibits muskets, bayonets, artillery fuse plugs, swords, field glasses, flags, the drum of a drummer boy, and pictures of very old veterans from Gettysburg's 75th anniversary in 1938.

If you really want to know more details of the Battle of Gettysburg, invest in a private, licensed guide from **Gettysburg National Military Park Guided Tours,** which can be arranged at the visitors center. You'll have to be serious about this since you'll need to rent a car to transport the guide who will take you on a personalized two-hour tour based on your interests. Great for real Civil War buffs, it's $70 for 7–15 people.

The option that seems to be the most popular with most people is the **Gettysburg Tour Center** (778 Baltimore St., 717/334-6296 or 800/447-8788, www. gettysburgbattlefieldtours.com) which

Gettysburg Battle Facts

It was a horrifying three days (or four, when you consider people were still being killed on July 4), and the scope of it still resonates nearly a century and a half later. The community survives on history, which is why facts like these are important to know:

Well over a century later, John Burns —the "Citizen Hero of Gettysburg"— stands ready with his rifle.

- Nearly seven million bullets were fired at Gettysburg by more than 160,000 soldiers. How many were Union, and how many Confederates? One park guide doesn't care. "They were *all* American soldiers," he explained.
- The oldest fighter was John Burns, the "Citizen Hero of Gettysburg." At 72, this veteran of the War of 1812 heard the commotion, got dressed in his blue swallowtail coat and top hat, grabbed his rifle, and started fighting alongside the fabled Iron Brigade on McPherson's Ridge. He was hit three times—the first bullet hit his belt buckle, the second his arm, and the third his ankle, which knocked him to the ground. Burying his ammo, he got up, limped towards home, and when confronted, he lied to Confederate soldiers that he was simply a farmer caught in the crossfire. They let him pass and he lived until 1872.
- In 1938, at the 75th anniversary of the battle, a 94-year-old veteran was asked if he was enjoying his stay in Gettysburg. "A lot more than I did 75 years ago," he said.
- In a letter home, one soldier wrote to his wife, "Soldiering is 99 percent boredom, and one percent sheer terror."
- At Gettysburg, more than 32,000 men were wounded, and 8,000 died. About 94 percent were killed by bullets, less than 1 percent by bayonet.
- Of the 1,328 monuments at Gettysburg, the best may be the Peace Memorial—the only one not dedicated to war. After the 50th anniversary of the battle in 1913, soldiers from the north and south pooled their own money and raised additional funds to create the monument built, not coincidentally, of Alabama limestone and Maine granite. The inscription, "Peace Eternal in a Nation United," says it all.

offers a fairly affordable way to get some good background information and a layout of the area. The $24.95 history lesson takes place aboard an open-air double-decker bus you would normally make fun of, but the schedule is punctual and the information factual (although little of it is presented with a great deal of creativity or enthusiasm). Still, it stops at historic sites such as Pickett's Charge and Bloody Run so you can take mental notes and return later to explore on your own. The departure point can vary based on the time of year, so call ahead.

Aside from a motorcycle, one of the coolest ways to see the Gettysburg battlefield is in a 1930s Yellowstone Park bus. **Historic Battlefield Bus Tours** (55 Steinwehr Ave., 717/334-8000, www.historictourcompany.com) offers 2.5-hour tours for about $20. The restored open-top classics are visually appealing and with only 17 passengers you'll get more attention.

If your bike is equipped with audio, you may want to skip the bus tour and trade $17.95 for a two-hour narrative CD tour of the battle's history that you can pick up at the **American Civil War Museum** (297 Steinwehr Ave., 717/334-6245, www.gettysburgmuseum.com). The narrative takes you through the battle's three days, telling you when to turn and where to look. The park itself offers a more affordable option: a free 90-minute podcast you can download and play as you take a walking tour. Check into that at **www.civilwartraveler.com.**

It's hard to believe World War II's most illustrious general could be overshadowed, but when Dwight Eisenhower bought a home in Gettysburg in 1950, he was destined to take a back seat to the battle. He used his farm here (the only home he ever owned) as a weekend retreat and temporary White House. Today, it is the **Eisenhower National Historic Site** (1195 Baltimore Pike, 717/338-9114, www.nps.gov/eise). If you grew up liking Ike, you'll like the tour ($7.50), which is available from the National Park Service Visitor Center. Access to the Eisenhower Farm is by shuttle bus only, so give your bike a rest in the center's parking lot. The displays are rich in personal items, such as Ike's World War II jacket and helmet.

Shopping

If your den looks suspiciously like a Civil War museum, then Gettysburg is where you'll want to stock up on items for the new wing. There are several impressive collectibles and antiquarian shops, including **The Union Drummer Boy** (13 Baltimore St., 717/334-2350, www.uniondb.com), which carries more memorabilia than a soldier carried in 1863: authentic muskets, carbines, artillery, revolvers, uniforms, swords, letters, leather goods, relics, artillery shells, flags, documents, bullets embedded in wood, and artifacts aplenty.

Blue-Plate Specials

The Lincoln Diner (32 Carlisle St., 717/334-3900) is just right for motorcycle travelers. An authentic 24-hour diner, it serves such staples as fried clams, fried oysters, breaded veal, and the obligatory cholesterol-rich breakfasts. Watch your diet at home, but this place may tempt you to pull an Elvis and pig out on a hot fudge banana royale.

Don't miss **Dunlap's** (90 Buford Ave., 717/334-4816, www.dunlapsrestaurant.com). It's been here forever, thanks to a menu that features ham, turkey, beef cooked and sliced on-site, fried chicken, real mashed potatoes, sandwiches, stuffed flounder, steaks, and big breakfasts. Dunlap's tops it off with cheap prices.

General Pickett's (571 Steinwehr Ave., 717/334-7580) is not a chain but a genuine honest-to-goodness buffet. Made-from-scratch soups, fresh-baked breads, a salad bar, and down-home entrées are all wrapped up with homemade pies and cakes. On the corner of the square, the **Plaza Restaurant** (28 Baltimore St., 717/334-1999, www.gettysburgplaza.com) also includes a lounge that's larger than the dining room. The specialty is Greek food (heroes, kebabs, souvlaki), but you can also go for steaks, crab legs, and homemade soups. Credit the lounge for keeping the joint jumpin' until 2:30 A.M.

Watering Holes

On the town square, **The Pub & Restaurant** (20–22 Lincoln Sq., 717/334-7100) gives you options: Head to the restaurant for a traditional entrée (chicken, steak, pasta, etc.) or buy a brew at the hammered copper-top bar. Popular with college students who like the $2 pitchers, the full bar also serves ales, domestic brews, and other spirits. If the weather's right, grab a sidewalk table and enjoy the evening and a cool one.

Also in the heart of downtown, the **Flying Bull Saloon** (28 Carlisle St., 717/334-6202), may be the best biker-style bar in town. Low-key and dark, it sets the stage with a pool table, darts, and a small stage for local bands. In addition to bar food, there are drink specials like Thursday's pitchers of Pabst for two bucks. Ah…college days.

As the name implies, the **Spring House Tavern** (89 Steinwehr Ave., 717/334-2100, www.dobbinhouse.com) is more like a colonial pub. In the basement of the Dobbin House, tavern waitresses wear colonial costumes, and candles light the room. Although it doubles as a family restaurant, the full bar, a handful of tap beers, and its unique setting make this place worth seeing.

Sharpshooters (900 Chambersburg Rd., 717/334-4332, www.sharpshootersgrille.

com) is a bar at the Inn at Herr Ridge. During the battle of Gettysburg, the home and outbuildings served as a Confederate hospital, but time and capitalism have turned it into a faithfully restored pre–Civil War tavern. Saloonkeepers serve beer straight from the ice into your sweaty hands. While the lounge is small and comfortable, a large deck can get you outdoors to enjoy the cool summer nights. In addition to bar food, entertainment varies from darts, foosball, and video games to a first for me: a black-light poolroom.

Shut-Eye

Numerous independent hotels are located near the battlefield, each offering similar rooms but different amenities—some feature a pool or whirlpool tub. In the heart of town, **Gettysburg Hotel** (1 Lincoln Sq., 717/337-2000 or 800/528-1234, www.hotelgettysburg.com, $99–153) is a full-service Best Western. This 1797 landmark has covered parking, a restaurant, and a few suites with fireplaces and whirlpool tubs. Their pub, McClellan's Tavern, is a popular watering hole.

Inn-dependence

For descriptions of and reservations for the majority of area inns, check **Inns of Gettysburg** (www.gettysburgbedandbreakfast.com).

Ride down the street to the **Farnsworth House Inn** (401 Baltimore St., 717/334-8838, www.farnsworthhouseinn.com, $145 and up), if you don't mind a gravel drive and the fact that a Confederate sharpshooter made this his post. The Victorian home has a sunroom and country garden breakfasts. It also offers a restaurant with dishes like country ham, peanut soup, meat casserole, and pumpkin fritters. Rumor has it some of the rooms are haunted, but the rates are the same with or without ghosts. Note: The

100 bullet holes in the house may make it slightly drafty in winter.

Traveling in a group? Looking for a place in the historic district? Consider **James Gettys Hotel** (27 Chambersburg St., 717/337-1334 or 888/900-5275, www.jamesgettyshotel.com, $145 and up). An inn in the 1830s, it served as a hostel and apartment house before being restored as an 11-room inn. Riders appreciate amenities including complimentary continental breakfasts and rooms and suites that sleep up to four. Suites include a kitchenette with microwave, refrigerator, coffeemakers, and two-burner stove.

A first-class option is the **Brickhouse Inn** (452 Baltimore St., 717/338-9337 or 800/864-3464, www.brickhouseinn.com, $109 and up). Equidistant between downtown and the visitor center, this place is a bargain when you consider the courtesy and service that culminates with an extraordinary breakfast served on the backyard patio. First-rate.

Chain Drive

These chain hotels are in town, or within 10 miles of the city center:

Best Western, Comfort Inn, Days Inn, Econo Lodge, Hampton Inn, Holiday Inn, Quality Inn, Red Carpet Inn, Sleep Inn, Super 8, Travelodge

For more information, including phone numbers and websites, see page 99.

SIDE TRIP: YORK HARLEY-DAVIDSON TOUR

Next to the Harley headquarters in Milwaukee, York (roughly 30 miles east of Gettysburg) is the site of most interest to riders. At more than 230 acres and with more than 1.5 million square feet under its roof, **Harley-Davidson's Final Assembly Plant** is the largest H-D facility, where more than 3,200 employees crank out 700 bikes a day. This tour is infinitely more interesting than a similar tour near the company headquarters.

Offered weekdays only (with Saturday tours added in summer) the one-hour factory tour begins as a guide takes you to the shop floor to view the parts manufacturing process and the final motorcycle assembly lines. It's absolutely cool to see strips of sheet metal stamped, pressed, and bent into fenders and fuel tanks. You'll follow the entire process and see how the component pieces are meshed with engines to create Softails, police bikes, cruisers, and special-order bikes. You can test-sit the newest models and spend as much time as you like in the renovated museum, which focuses on the history, people, process, and product in the York factory. Tours are offered on a first-come first-served basis, arrive early. Tours depart between 9 A.M.–2 P.M., with the tour center and gift shop open 8 A.M.–4 P.M. Call 717/848-1177 or 877/883-1450 for tour times and availability. Reservations are required for groups of 10 or more, call 717/852-6590. The York Visitor Center (at the plant) can be reached at 717/852-6006. On the tour, you'll need to wear close-toed shoes and leave your camera behind—so don't get any ideas about starting your own motorcycle corporation. The plant is off U.S. 30 at 1425 Eden Road, one mile east of I-83.

ON THE ROAD: GETTYSBURG TO LEESBURG

Even though it'll be a short run to Leesburg, don't plan on leaving late since the roads ahead are beautiful and peaceful and you'll be racing the sun if you decide to stop in Catoctin, Antietam, or Harper's Ferry. Try to give yourself a full day to enjoy the country.

U.S. 15 Business Route South, the level two-lane road leaving Gettysburg, passes statuary and monuments that suggest that the entire town is a cemetery. Just past the town limits, **Rider's Edge** (2490 Emmitsburg Rd., 717/334-2518) is a convenient stop for last-minute gear. About six miles later, you'll approach the Mason-Dixon line as you hook up with U.S. 15 South, which turns into a larger highway, albeit narrower than an interstate. Although this is no back road, it provides surprisingly nice vistas of farmland and continues over the Maryland state line before Route 77 West veers off to the right and positions you for one of the great rides.

Your disappointment over leaving U.S. 15 dissipates the moment you enter Maryland's **Catoctin Mountain Park.** Among America's top roads, this is one that you can ride like an animal. This two-lane exclamation point is a thrill-a-minute road that rolls past valleys, twists, lakes, sharp curves, deer, and rivers. Past Pryor's Orchards (purveyor of jelly, honey, nuts, and apples), you'll spot a great river and a setting as intriguing as Sherwood Forest. Glance up and the mountain peaks reveal themselves well above the forest. Look ahead and the road is a grab bag of mild curves and sharp edges, like an abridged version of New Hampshire's Kank. There are side roads leading deeper into the park, so if you have time to spare, get lost and you may stumble across a waterfall or wind up at the gates of Camp David. When you return to Route 77 where the sun dapples through the branches above, the road is intersected by the legendary Appalachian Trail. This marks the point where a steep descent weaves down the hill.

Too soon, you're out of the woods. Instead of continuing into the traffic of Hagerstown, turn left on Route 66 and drop south toward the town of Sharpsburg and the Antietam battlefield. The road is marked by apple orchards and hand-painted signs announcing bales of straw for sale, and a few miles down there's a general store in Mount Aetna where you can pull over for a soda pop. By the time you reach the junction at I-70, you'll be content to blow past it because you're sure there are far better roads ahead. There are. Ahead the asphalt is as fluid as a river, leading to farmland vistas and bucolic countryside, bumps and small hills, and sweeping turns that throw you into great straightaways.

At Boonsboro, the roads T's at Alternate U.S. 40 and you take a funky fork south and ride several blocks to get on Route 34 West. Soon you'll be on the Sharpsburg Pike, and although the route switches direction often, you'll pass villages and avoid cities and have a blast all the way to Sharpsburg. When you hit the intersection at Route 65, turn right and ride about two miles to the **Antietam National Battlefield** (301/432-5124, www.nps.gov/anti, $4). Sadly, even more than the events of September 11, 2001, this site marks the bloodiest day in American history. When Lee made his first invasion to take the war into the North, he brought 40,000 troops. General George B. McClellan led more than 80,000 Union soldiers. When they met on September 17, 1862—a year before the Battle of Gettysburg—more than 23,000 men were left dead, wounded, or missing. To learn more, watch a film in the visitor center's theater: There's an introductory film shown daily on the hour or a one-hour documentary about the battle shown daily at noon. The loop road will lead you on a self-guided tour that's just over eight miles with 11 stops along the way, or, for a fee, tour guides who know much more than a brochure can be retained through www.antietambattlefieldguides.com.

Next, prepare yourself for a weirdly wild ride. From Route 65, return to Route 34 and turn right, where a block later, Mechanic Street is on your left. Turn here. Soon this will become Harpers Ferry Road and soon it will become a road you love. Almost immediately, there are oddly angled cornfields creating nice dips, and sharp curves and slow curves wrapping around stone walls and cornstalks. This blacktop roller coaster hauls you up a hill, slings you one way at the peak, and then drops and lifts you up again before slinging you the other way.

White churches and cemeteries mark the road, and new sights flash past: bales of hay, the stone bridges, the one-lane bridge that's perfect for a photo, the river, and the valley that gives you a sense of cosmic proportion since it all seems nearly void of life, save for a few homes that pockmark the woods. Somewhere along the way, there's a very tricky and very important fork near a blip of a community called Samples Manor; although, you can turn left or right here and end up in the same place. I swung to the right to stay on Harpers Ferry Road and continued south toward Pleasantville, riding through miles of desolate primeval forest where the lack of civilization convinced me that I had ridden off the face of the earth. Just about the time you'd be tempted to shoot up a signal flare, you'll spy the Potomac peeking through the narrow woods to your right. You'll merge onto Sandyhook Road in a ramshackle riverside town that looks like coal-mining country—without the coal. File away a mental image, roll under a bridge, make a buttonhook turn to reach that same bridge (U.S. 340), and cross into Virginia.

Follow U.S. 340 West for a minute or two and you'll be in West Virginia and at the visitor center of **Harpers Ferry National Historical Park** (304/535-6029,

www.nps.gov/hafe, $6). A must-see stop, this is where radical abolitionist John Brown, hoping to jump-start a slave rebellion, rounded up 18 slaves and attacked the U.S. Army arsenal in October 1859. Didn't happen. However, the Civil War *did* happen—and because of its placement where the Shenandoah and Potomac rivers meet, during the Civil War this town (like Liz Taylor) changed hands eight times. There is not a single museum here. Instead, there are 25 museums in a park that spans three states: West Virginia, Virginia, and Maryland. You'll see a restored town, hiking trails, guided tours, interpretive tours, and living history programs. While the park is open all year, most programs are held in the spring and summer.

From Harpers Ferry, double back on U.S. 340 so you can eye the ruggedly handsome Shenandoah River. Ahead, Route 671 is the continuation of Harpers Ferry Road where you turn right at the well-stocked service station. You'll gather that Virginia must have gotten a good price on scenery, because there's far more of it here than in Addis Ababa. Later, you may see evidence of the state's wildflower program, which blankets highway medians with flowers, such as black-eyed Susans, daffodils, goldenrod, and ox-eye daisies.

Route 671 is a fast two-lane road, with pretty valleys and canopy roads that are in direct contrast to the sharp twists, weaves, ascents, and descents you'll be making. Although McMansions threaten what was once unspoiled scenery, the road's all right and lasts about eight miles until you reach Route 9 (aka Charles Town Pike). Turn left at a little country store and head towards Leesburg on Route 9, taking a well-deserved break to see great stone walls stretched across fields, farmhouses dotting the tops of low hills, and cornfields everywhere. If it's dusk and the conditions are right, you may have the pleasure of watching a great gray fog rolling in over the hills.

Shortly, Route 9 merges with Route 7. It's been a great ride, and now it's time to head east and rest up in Leesburg.

LEESBURG PRIMER

Anyone who's heard of the Civil War has heard the oft-repeated phrase describing it as "brother against brother." To see how true that is, this reality was embodied in the area surrounding Leesburg.

After John Brown's raid on Harpers Ferry in 1859, folks in Loudoun County feared a slave insurrection. And even though this was never the site of a major battle or even a significant skirmish, in May 1861 Leesburg voted 400–22 to secede from the Union. Just a few miles away, the Germans and Quakers of Waterford voted 220–31 to remain with, *and fight for,* the preservation of the United States. Thus, the area spawned Virginia's only organized Union force: the Loudoun Rangers, led by Quaker Sam Meade, who scouted, patrolled, and skirmished with Confederate forces in the area.

These conflicts are no longer apparent as today's lifestyle reflects a more genteel history. And though this may not be the most historical town you'll stay in, it's worth an overnight on your way south.

ON THE ROAD: LEESBURG

Leesburg is just right for a bike ride. Downtown, which is at the intersection of Market Street (Rte. 7) and King Street (U.S. 15), is a manageable size; there's plenty of parking for bikes, and the diners, nightclubs, and riders from assorted clubs are visible reminders that you're in the right place.

If your interests lean towards obtaining a quick and painless history lesson, for just three bucks head inside the **Loudoun Museum** (16 Loudoun St., 703/777-7427, www.loudounmuseum.org). A smart first stop, you can always count on the short video that explains the history of Loudoun county and the Battle of Ball's Bluff, a small but important skirmish that represents the first and largest conflict fought in Leesburg. Between May and October, there are historical walking tours ($10) available by reservation if you have the desire to learn even more about Leesburg's participation in the Civil War or, as the locals call it, "the War of Northern Aggression." All in all, it's a nice museum that also includes slices of colonial history and information on local farmer John Binns who, in 1804, wrote a "Treatise on Practical Farming." This introduction to modern farming techniques (some of which are still in use) drew praise from the king of gentleman farmers, Thomas Jefferson.

The remainder of downtown is like a smaller Charleston; the houses have been

Cruising across the Potomac with *White's Ferry:* a short trip that creates a lot of memories.

preserved well, although their scale is not as impressive. Cluttered antiques shops abound. If shopping's not your thing, take U.S. 15 a mile north to Battlefield Parkway and see Ball's Bluff Battlefield and then attend to a plan more important than investing in your 401(k). Think about shoving some grub in a saddlebag and then ride up U.S. 15 to White's Ferry Road where you turn east and follow a narrow path to the water. Scratch around for four bucks (seven bucks round-trip) and board **White's Ferry** (24801 White's Ferry Rd., 301/349-5200) for a short and enjoyable ferry ride over the wide and tranquil Potomac River. When you reach Maryland a few minutes later, park it and enjoy a picnic—an inexpensive pleasure that feels like a million bucks.

PULL IT OVER: LEESBURG HIGHLIGHTS
Attractions and Adventures

What happened at **Ball's Bluff Battlefield** (Battlefield Pkwy., 703/779-9372) marks a significant day in Civil War history. In 1861, Union troops were convinced it wouldn't be long before they'd whip the Rebels into submission. But after 1,700 Union soldiers crossed the Potomac and came face to face with an equally determined 1,700 Confederate troops defending Leesburg, they changed their minds. When the smoke cleared, there were 155 Rebel casualties—which was a pittance compared to the Union's 900-plus casualties representing men who were shot, drowned, wounded, and captured. Even worse, bodies of the drowned men floated downstream to bring the reality of the war to the front door of Washington, D.C. The stinging defeat had some benefits: A committee was formed to investigate Union defeats and corruption and to tighten up the war effort. There's a park

and cemetery here, as well as a mile-long hiking loop with interpretive signs that help you follow the battle. On weekends between May and October, free tours are given.

At Butts/BTI Whitewater (10985 Harpers Ferry Rd., Purcellville, 540/668-9007 or 800/836-9911, www.btiwhitewater.com), they rent two sizes of inner tubes ($19–30), with the option of renting a companion cooler that floats in its own inner tube. Genius! Leave your bike behind, because Butts will bus you up the Shenandoah River, tell you where to get off in Maryland, and then let you drift for two hours and over three rapids before meeting you back in Ol' Virginny for the bus ride home.

Loudoun County, the area surrounding Leesburg, is a rider's paradise. There are dozens of back roads and scenic byways lined with stone-stacked fences, horse farms, vineyards, and towns and villages steeped in history. If it looks like wine country, you're right. You can pick up a map of the Loudoun Wine Trail and the county's vineyards and attractions from the **Loudoun County (Leesburg) Visitors Center** (112-G South St. SE, 703/771-2617 or 800/752-6118, www.visitloudoun.org). There's evidence of this at **Leesburg Vintner** (29 S. King St., 703/777-3322, www.leesburgvintner.com), which has been recognized as Virginia's wine retailer of the year. You'll find barrels of wine (cleverly packaged in bottles), as well as gourmet picnic foods like cheese, crackers, peanuts and other Virginia products.

Blue-Plate Specials

Leesburg Restaurant (9 S. King St., 703/777-3292) serves breakfast, lunch, and dinner daily. In the morning, an equal number of riders and locals appear to frequent this place, a down-home restaurant since 1865. I think this is where Grant threw his victory party.

The perfectly named **Mighty Midget Kitchen** (202 Harrison St. SE #A, 703/779-7880) was crafted out of the fuselage of a World War II–era B-29 bomber. A downtown Leesburg institution since 1947, it serves something called a "hamburger doner" (a German-style hamburger), as well as hot dogs, fries, and soda pop. There's indoor and outdoor patio seating as well as beer and wine served in a *beirgarten* setting.

For a nicer meal, there's none nicer than at the **Tuscarora Mill** (203 Harrison St., 703/771.9300, www.tuskies.com), which, oddly enough, is built within the shell of an old 1899 mill. Coincidence? It's not something I do often, but splurging on something other than diner food can be a nice reward, and entrées like smoked chicken pasta, sesame roasted Atlantic salmon, and a strip steak, plus a nice lounge, can be the perfect conclusion to a long day's ride.

Watering Holes

Although Leesburg seems to have an upscale veneer, it's not above supporting a biker bar in the heart of town. The **Downtown Saloon** (7 N. King St., 703/669-3090) has been around since 1965 perhaps because there are no additives—just a love of motorcycling and the three Ps: peanuts, pinups, and pool. Come here to enjoy bar food, live bands, and a comfortable setting where you can kick back and map out the next leg. As you enjoy your brew, look at the county courthouse through the window and consider the sign that reads "Better off here than across the street."

The **Kings Court Tavern** (2C Loudoun St. SW, 703/777-7747) is less biker than Brit. A pub theme runs throughout, with private booths, a long bar, TVs, and liquor.

Downstairs at **Ball's Bluff** (2D Loudoun St. SW, 703/777-7757), the underground pub features a well-stocked bar, darts, occasional live music, and traditional food, such as wings, sandwiches, and salads.

Shut-Eye
Inn-dependence

The **Loudoun County B&B Guild** (www.loudounbandb.com) represents many inns throughout the county, as does the county itself—www.visitloudoun.org. One close to downtown is the **Norris House Inn** (108 Loudoun St. SW, 703/777-1806 or 800/644-1806, www.norrishouse.com, $125 and up). This inn features a parlor, a library, a sunroom, and a rambling verandah overlooking the gardens. Antiques accent guest rooms, some of which have fireplaces. The downside: Parking's in a garage a few blocks away.

Chain Drive

These chain hotels are in town, or within 10 miles of the city center:

Best Western, Hampton Inn, Holiday Inn, Ramada

For more information, including phone numbers and websites, see page 99.

ON THE ROAD: LEESBURG TO FREDERICKSBURG

Unlike Wild West desert straightaways where you can strap your handlebars in place and take a nap, roads in Virginia demand your attention. That's the good part. The downside is that the ride to reach Fredericksburg is enjoyable, but it isn't flawless. This is the route I chose because it was largely the most direct and easy to follow, but don't hesitate exploring the nest of back roads on your own.

Leave Leesburg on U.S. 15, the same road that leads out of Gettysburg. It's not impressive at first, just an ordinary road with an ordinary job. But about a dozen miles later at Gilbert's Corner, turn right and ride on U.S. 50 west toward Aldie, followed by Middleburg. If you follow U.S. 50 for another 3,000 miles, you'd reach Sacramento, California. There are beautiful horse farms here, and if you owned an Arabian instead of a bike, you'd probably move in. The passion for all things equestrian is omnipresent in this area and the people shopping in the upscale uptown district of Middleburg are clearly devoted to horses—you can see it in their faces.

When you leave Middleburg behind, turning left to take County Road 626 (aka Halfway Road) south, nothing is sudden. The road reads like a book, revealing a little at a time until the whole story is right in front of you, and here the subject is open Virginia land. When you reach the Plains (which ain't too fancy), look for a service station and then some smooth country riding—nice shallow dips, split-rail fences, sweeping curves, weeping willows, and rustic homes.

Take Route 245, a nice road that crosses beneath I-66, turns into U.S. 17, and then veers off to your left on U.S. 15/29 to bypass Warrenton. Eventually you'll ride into small towns like Remington and ride out seconds later looking for Route 651 toward Sumerduck, a remote road that mixes things up with some tight twists, graceful curves, inclines, and one-lane bridges. From here, the roads are country, and you get the strong feeling you're entering the South. You are. Within a few miles, you've switched channels from *Masterpiece Theatre* to *Hee-Haw*. It's hard to believe this change in cultures happens less than an hour's drive from the nation's capital.

When Route 651 rejoins U.S. 17, turn right and follow it to Fredericksburg, one of the nicest towns you'll have the pleasure to meet.

FREDERICKSBURG PRIMER

Why was Fredericksburg so vital to Civil War soldiers? Open a map, put your finger on this city, and you'll be pointing midway between the Confederate capital of Richmond and the Union capital of Washington, D.C. With that and the high banks of the Rappahannock River providing a natural defensive barrier, as well as a rail corridor capable of keeping both armies supplied, the desire to hold the town led to four separate battles fought in and around the city.

How bad did it get? Consider that Fredericksburg changed hands 10 times during the war and left more than 100,000 casualties with 85,000 men wounded and 15,000 men killed. Add it up and that's more casualties than in the three previous wars (the Mexican–American War, the War of 1812, and the Revolutionary War) *combined*. Needless to say, Fredericksburg was considered the bloodiest landscape in America.

Fortunately, since the Civil War the town has never been reduced to that level of horror. Today, a good vibe runs throughout Fredericksburg where the residents are friendly and the pace is slow, and it all goes a long way in making this one of your most rewarding stops. Along with a sense of history, folks have a sense of humor, so certain tours are far more enjoyable than any I've seen elsewhere. Add to this a walkable downtown district filled with restaurants, art, and antiques-filled shops and you've arrived at the perfect base to reach other Civil War sites, such as Spotsylvania to the east or the Stonewall Jackson Shrine to the south.

ON THE ROAD: FREDERICKSBURG

Of all the historical towns I've visited, I'd say Fredericksburg does the best job of making history interesting and entertaining without turning it into a Disney cartoon caricature.

To get started, park your bike, put on some walking shoes, and do the town. At a good clip you can see it all in a day, although I'd wager you may want to stick around a little longer. For about eight blocks, both sides of Caroline Street provide numerous diversions from cheap antiques to a cool diner to historic homes.

Swing by the **Fredericksburg Visitor Center** (706 Caroline St., 540/373-1776) to buy tickets for everything historical in town, such as the Hugh Mercer Apothecary Shop, the Rising Sun Tavern, Mary Washington House, and Fredericksburg/Spotsylvania National Military Park. These tours are a must while you're here, and buying a Day Pass will save you 40 percent over the price of individual tickets. The center also has great maps for walking tours that highlight different eras of the town's history. If you'd rather save the shoe leather, **Trolley Tours of Fredericksburg** (706 Caroline St., 540/898-0737, www.fredericksburgtrolley. com) departs for a tour of historic homes, attractions, and the famous Sunken Road. In addition to seeing Federal, Confederate, and the nation's oldest Masonic cemeteries, it's a smart way to get a lay of the land and know where to return to on your bike.

On foot, just head north on Caroline Street and allow time to drop into shops along the way. At the corner of Caroline and Amelia Streets, step into the **Hugh Mercer Apothecary Shop** (1020 Caroline St. 540/375-3362, open daily, $5). Running the shop while the good doctor is out, docents dressed as colonial-era wenches demonstrate the "modern medicines" the doc uses to treat patients. The kick is that they never break character, even while discussing the medicinal value of leeches, herbs, amputations, mustard plasters, and a "good puking." With the right person playing the role, this is one of the most fun tours you'll find. If you're a doctor, you'll have plenty to talk to your peers about. If you're a lawyer, you'll find plenty of times to think *malpractice.*

About three blocks north at the **Rising**

Confederate soldier Richard Kirkland, moved by the anguished cries of the enemy at Fredericksburg, scaled a protective wall to aid the dying. When soldiers held their fire, he became known as "The Angel of Marye's Heights." This sculpture was created by Felix George Weihs De Weldon in 1965.

Sun Tavern (1304 Caroline St., 540/371-1494), the format is the same and just as entertaining. Anywhere else, this would be a brief walk through an old building. Not here. The Rising Sun Tavern was built in 1760 by Charles Washington, the younger brother of George Washington, and, quite likely, the Billy Carter of Colonial America. You can learn a lot here—for example, tavern decks had only 51 cards. You had to pay one shilling, sixpence for the 52nd card. Otherwise, you were not "dealing with a full deck."

After checking out the remaining historical sites, hop on your bike and ride to the **Fredericksburg Battlefield** (1013 Lafayette Blvd., 540/373-6122, www.nps. gov/frsp). Although the museum is much smaller than the one at Gettysburg, the introductory video does a good job of explaining the battles that happened here. When you exit out the back door, a self-guided tour starts at the Sunken Road, which feels like one of the saddest places in America. In December 1862, Confederate soldiers sheltered behind a high stone wall above the road were able to cut down Union troops like lambs at the slaughter.

It must have been a brutal scene, but a monument a little farther down may restore a bit of your faith in humanity. The monument is dedicated to Richard Kirkland, a 19-year-old Confederate soldier who couldn't bear to hear the dying cries of the enemy. He jumped the wall and ran to the aid of the suffering men, giving them water from his canteen. How'd he survive the crossfire? Both Confederate and Union soldiers held their fire while he was on his mission of mercy.

There you go. Another bit of history and heroism thanks to the man known as "The Angel of Marye's Heights." From here it's time to wrap up your tour with a nice dinner and a quiet evening at your inn.

PULL IT OVER: FREDERICKSBURG HIGHLIGHTS
Attractions and Adventures

Collectively, the **Fredericksburg/Spotsylvania National Military Park** maintains nearly 6,000 acres of land and admission to all local battlefields as well as the Stonewall Jackson shrine is free. Both the **Fredericksburg Battlefield Visitor Center** (1013 Lafayette Blvd., 540/373-6122, www.nps.gov/frsp) and **Chancellorsville Battlefield Visitor Center** (Rte. 3 W., 540/786-2880) help interpret the four battlefields: Fredericksburg, Chancellorsville, The Wilderness, and Spotsylvania Courthouse.

More history is found at the **Fredericksburg Area Museum** (907 Princess Anne St., 540/371-3037, www.famcc.org, $7), housed in two buildings. The museum contains an assortment of Civil War weapons in an old 1860 Town Hall/Market House that survived Civil War battles. Within a Beaux-Arts building, there's an interesting collection from Fredericksburg's own history.

It turns out that the Father of our Country also had a Brother-in-Law of our Country, and that was Colonel Fielding Lewis who married George's sister, Betty. She and Fielding lived at **Kenmore Plantation & Gardens** (1201 Washington Ave., 540/373-3381, www.kenmore.org) which Washington himself surveyed when the land was part of a 1,300-acre plantation. Guides claim that an award given for the home's plasterwork ranks this among one of the most beautiful houses in America (a bit of an overstatement since the honor was given in the 1930s). Worth it if you're a fan of Washington's (or presidential sisters), the tour can drag so it's an $8 crapshoot.

If you left your dulcimer at home, one of the neatest shops in Fredericksburg is **Picker's Supply** (902 Caroline St., 540/371-4669 or 800/830-4669, www.pickerssupply.com). Even if you don't play, you will be tempted to pick up a banjo, mandolin, or fiddle for the road. If you do jam, check out the vintage guitars.

Blue-Plate Specials

The reason why you may be drawn to **Goolrick's** (901 Caroline St., 540/373-3411) is that it's the oldest continuously operating soda fountain in America. Open daily for breakfast, lunch, and dinner, Goolrick's features an abridged menu of sandwiches, soups, homemade macaroni and potato salad, and fresh-squeezed lemonade. A great old-fashioned flashback, it's a neat place to order up a thick milkshake and imagine you're still in high school.

Here since 1960, **Anne's Grill** (1609 Princess Anne St., 540/373-9621) is a testament to simple meals and superior service. Big home cooking, breakfast all day, burgers, steaks, seafood at lunch and dinner, sassy waitresses, and lots of locals. Anne's Grill is closed on Wednesdays and 2–4:30 P.M. daily.

Anne's counterpart is down the street at the **2400 Diner** (2400 Princess Anne St., 540/373-9049). For more than half a century, it, too, has been serving good dishes done right. There's a little bit of everything here, from subs and chicken to steaks and fish—ah, the pleasure of road food. The diner's open 7 A.M.–9 P.M. Monday–Saturday, and until 3 P.M. Sunday.

Watering Holes

When you visit **J. Brian's Tap Room** (200 Hanover St., 540/373-0738, www.jbrianstaproom.com), you may be drinking shoulder to shoulder with D.C. politicians. Photos show that this place attracts a mix of conservative and liberal imbibers.

Why not? It's a cool place with 20 beers on tap, including Woodchuck Cider and Bass Ale. Happy hour lasts 4–7 P.M., and the Wurlitzer jukebox is authentic. Oh, yeah—George Washington once owned this place.

Shut-Eye

Fredericksburg has several inns, but if you prefer the modern conveniences of a TV, large bed, and private bath, you may do better at a chain hotel. Call the visitors center for current listings.

Motels and Motor Courts

The **Inn at Olde Silk Mill** (1707 Princess Anne St., 540/371-5666, www.innattheoldesilkmill.com, $89–159) was once an old motel, but has been upgraded, with rooms and suites accented with Civil War antiques. A complimentary continental breakfast is included.

Inn-dependence

The **Richard Johnston Inn** (711 Caroline St., 540/899-7606 or 877/557-0770, www.therichardjohnstoninn.com, $105 and up weekdays, $135 and up weekends) features seven rooms and two suites, some of them uncommonly large, many filled with antiques and reproductions, and all with a private bath. Built in the late 1700s, the inn has a great spot in the heart of downtown, with generous parking and a full breakfast.

Chain Drive

These chain hotels are in town, or within 10 miles of the city center: **Best Western, Comfort Inn, Econo Lodge, Hampton Inn, Hilton, Holiday Inn, Howard Johnson, Motel 6, Quality Inn, Ramada, Residence Inn, Sleep Inn, Super 8, Travelodge** For more information, including phone numbers and websites, see page 99.

Resources for Riders

Civil War Run

Maryland Travel Information
Maryland Tourism—866/639-3526, www.visitmaryland.org

Pennsylvania Travel Information
Pennsylvania Road Conditions—866/976-8747, www.paturnpike.com
Pennsylvania State Parks—888/727-2757, www.dcnr.state.pa.us
Pennsylvania Tourism and Lodging Information—717/232-8880,
    www.patourism.org
Pennsylvania Visitor Information—800/847-4872, www.visitpa.com

Virginia Travel Information
Virginia Camping—800/933-7275, www.dcr.state.va.us
Virginia Civil War Trails—888/248-4592, www.civilwartrails.org
Virginia Highway Helpline—800/367-7623
Virginia Tourism—800/847-4882, www.virginia.org

Local and Regional Information
Fredericksburg Visitor Center—540/373-1776 or 800/678-4748, www.visitfred.com
Gettysburg Convention and Visitors Bureau—717/339-0767 or 800/337-5015,
    www.gettysburgcvb.org
Loudoun County (Leesburg) Visitors Center—703/771-2617 or 800/752-6118,
    www.visitloudoun.org

Pennsylvania Motorcycle Shops
Action Motorsports—1881 Whiteford Rd., York, 717/757-2688,
    www.actionmotorsportsyork.com
Battlefield Harley-Davidson/Buell—21 Cavalry Field Rd., Gettysburg,
    717/337-9005 or 877/595-9005, www.battlefieldharley-davidson.com
Don's Kawasaki—20 E. Market St., Hallam (York), 717/755-6002,
    www.donskawasaki.com
Hanover Powersports—717/632-8801, 1754 Carlisle Pike, Hanover,
    www.hanovercycles.com
Laugermans Harley-Davidson—100 Arsenal Rd., York, 717/854-3214,
    www.laugerman.com
Motosports—2117 Baltimore Pike (Rte. 94 S), Hanover, 717/632-7093,
    www.motosportsinc.com
Riders Edge Yamaha—2490 Emmitsburg Rd., Gettysburg, 717/334-2518,
    www.ridersedgeyamaha.com

(continued next page)

Resources for Riders (continued)

Virginia Motorcycle Shops

Battlefield Motorcycles—1103 Lafayette Blvd., Fredericksburg, 540/371-7433

Extreme Powersports—10725 Courthouse Rd., Fredericksburg, 540/891-4009,
www.extremepowersport.com

Fredericksburg Motorsports—430 Kings Hwy., Fredericksburg, 540/899-9100
or 888/899-9129, www.youroneforfun.com

Loudoun Motorsports—212 Catoctin Circle SE, Leesburg, 703/777-1652,
www.loudounmotorsports.com

Morton's BMW—5099A Jefferson Davis Hwy., Fredericksburg, 540/891-9844,
www.mortonsbmw.com

Resources

MOTORCYCLE WEBSITES

Great American Motorcycle Tours
www.motorcycleamerica.com
Partner site for this book, with abridged ride descriptions, photographs, and links.

Moto-Directory
www.moto-directory.com
Perhaps the best bike site, with roughly 10,000 links to events, rallies, magazines, videos, tours, stolen bike reports, riding clubs, rental operators, dealers, and salvage yards.

Motorcycle Roads—1
www.motorcycleroads.us
Super site with recommendations from riders on popular and seldom traveled roads across America, viewable state-by-state. Links for submitting your favorites and finding travel resources.

Motorcycle Roads—2
www.motorcycleroads.com
Nationwide guide with recommended rides and tours listed state-by-state, graded by scenery, road quality, and roadside amenities, activities, and attractions.

Motorcycle-USA
www.motorcycle-usa.com
News, product reviews, bike tests, photo galleries, classifieds, message boards, and ride ratings.

Trader Online
www.cycletrader.com
The online version of the popular *Trader* magazines. Search by model, size, year, price, location, etc.

Harley-Davidson Links
www.hdlinks.com
Connections to H-D and other American motorcycle related sites.

Motorcycle Accessories Warehouse
800/241-2222
www.accwhse.com
Parts, supplies, and thousands of links to clothes and closeouts, from goggles to tank covers.

Motorcycle Online
www.motorcycle.com
Digital motorcycle magazine with bikes, products, reviews, videos, clubs, events, how-tos, rides, classifieds, financing, and chats.

Rider Magazine
www.ridermagazine.com
Links to *Rider* and *American Rider* magazines, archives, and ride maps.

Sport-Touring
www.sport-touring.net
Extensive discussion forum for tour, tech, and sales information.

SELECTED MANUFACTURERS

Most manufacturers' sites will lead to showrooms, accessories, clothing, riders clubs, FAQs, dealers, and riding products.

BMW
800/831-1117
www.bmwmotorcycles.com

Buell
www.buell.com

Ducati
www.ducati.com

Harley-Davidson
800/258-2464
www.harley-davidson.com

Honda
310/532-9811 or 866/784-1870
www.hondamotorcycle.com

Kawasaki
800/661-7433
www.kawasaki.com

Moto Guzzi
www.motoguzzi.it

Suzuki
www.suzukicycles.com

Triumph
678/854-2010
www.triumph.co.uk

Victory
www.victory-usa.com

Yamaha
800/889-2624
www.yamaha-motor.com

SELECTED MOTORCYCLE ORGANIZATIONS

American Motorcyclist Association
800/262-5646
www.ama-cycle.org
If you belong to one motorcycling organization, make it the AMA. The association sponsors thousands of sanctioned events and provides a monthly magazine, trip routing, hotel discounts, and club information for approximately 250,000 members.

Motorcycle Events Association
727/343-1049 or 866/203-4485
www.motorcycleevents.com
Provides information on Daytona, Sturgis, Laconia, and other major rallies as well as charity rides and motorcycle shows across America.

Motorcycle Product News
800/722-8764
www.mpnmag.com
Lists products, distributors, manufacturers, parts, and accessories; primarily used by dealers and rental operators.

Motorcycle Riders Foundation
202/546-0983 or
800/673-5646
www.mrf.org
Lobbying group for riders' rights, with links.

Motorcycle Safety Foundation
800/446-9227
www.msf-usa.org
Offers safe riding courses throughout the United States; participation can lower your insurance rates. Also features information on rider training and industry contacts.

SELECTED RIDING CLUBS
American Gold Wing Association
www.agwa.com

Blue Knights
207/947-4600 or 877/254-5362
www.blueknights.org

BMW Motorcycle Owners of America
636/394-7277
www.bmwmoa.org

Christian Motorcyclists Association
870/389-6196
www.cmausa.org

Gold Wing Road Riders Association
623/581-2500 or 800/843-9460
www.gwrra.org

Harley Owners Group
800/258-2464
www.hog.com

Honda Riders Club of America
800/847-4722
www.hrca.honda.com

Motorcycle Clubs & Associations
www.moto-directory.com/clubs.asp

Riders of Kawasaki
877/765-2582
www.kawasaki.com/rok

Women on Wheels
800/322-1969
www.womenonwheels.org

SELECTED RALLIES
Each year across the country, there are thousands of rallies of all shapes and sizes. Here are links to some of the largest—visit their websites for upcoming dates. Most rally sites include information on registration, rides, vendors, lodging, histories, and entertainment.

Americade Motorcycle Rally
518/798-7888
www.tourexpo.com
Lake George, New York

Bikes, Blues & BBQ Motorcycle Rally
479/527-9993
www.bikesbluesandbbq.org
Fayetteville, Arkansas

Bike Week and Biketoberfest
386/255-0981 (Bike Week)
www.officialbikeweek.com
386/255-0415 or 800/854-1234
(Biketoberfest)
www.biketoberfest.org
Daytona Beach, Florida

Laconia Rally
603/366-2000
www.laconiamcweek.com
Laconia, New Hampshire

Sturgis Rally and Races
605/720-0800
www.sturgismotorcyclerally.com
Sturgis, South Dakota

SELECTED MOTORCYCLE RENTAL COMPANIES

California Motorcycle Rentals
858/456-9577
www.calif-motorcyclerental.com

EagleRider Motorcycle Rental
310/536-6777 or 888/900-9901
www.eaglerider.com
Nationwide service, renting fully equipped Road Kings, Softails, Fat Boys, and Electra Glides. Locations in America, Mexico, and Europe. Also conducts tours.

Harley Motorcycle Rental
415/456-9910 or 888/812-9253
www.motohaven.net
Novato, California

Motorcycle Rental Resource Page
www.harleys.com/mrrp.html
Rental operators listed by state.

Route 66 Riders Motorcycle Rentals
310/578-0112 or 888/434-4473
www.route66riders.com
Marina Del Ray, California

GENERAL TRAVEL INFORMATION

Historic Hotels of America
800/678-8946
www.historichotels.org
Affiliated with the National Trust for Historic Preservation, HHA is a diverse collection of uniquely American lodgings, from rustic inns to elegant hotels. Rates at these member properties may be on the high end, but if you split the costs, you may do all right.

Kampgrounds of America (KOA)
www.koa.com
Information on more than 500 campgrounds nationwide.

Mad Maps
www.madmaps.com
Superb, informative motorcycle maps custom-designed to highlight scenic roads and popular routes across the country.

MapQuest
www.mapquest.com
Trip planning, route, and mileage information.

National Forest Service
www.fs.fed.us
Links to national forests and campgrounds.

National Parks Camping Reservations
800/436-7275 or 877/444-6777
www.recreation.gov
A one-call-books-all national company that handles reservations for 45,000 campsites at 1,700 national forest campgrounds across America. Books for most national parks, but does not include state parks.

National Park Foundation
202/354-6460 or 888/467-2757
www.nationalparks.org
Partner site of America's national parks, designed to introduce you to the parks and assist in trip-planning.

National Park Service

www.nps.gov
Central point for links to parks and recreation, history and culture, nature, science, interpretation, and education.

Road Conditions

www.usroadconditions.com
Links to information on road conditions in every state.

Road Trip USA

www.roadtripusa.com
Eleven cross-country riding routes to get you off the beaten path and onto pre-interstate roads.

Scenic Byways

www.byways.org
An excellent site detailing thousands of miles of scenic byways and back roads across the nation. Also offers links for trip-planning and personal journals.

State Motorcycle and Helmet Laws

www.amadirectlink.com/legisltn/laws.asp

State and National Park Links

www.llbean.com/parksearch

State Parks

www.stateparks.com
Comprehensive state-by-state listing with contact information, links, and information on hundreds of state parks.

State Park Reservations

www.reserveamerica.com
Facilitates campsite reservations for many state and private parks and campgrounds in North America.

Weather Channel

www.weather.com

ROAD TIPS

America the Beautiful Pass

Each year, America's National Parks are visited more than 265 million times, a figure totaling more fans and guests than visit NFL games, Disney parks, and Universal Studios attractions combined. If you plan to visit more than one national park, invest in the National Parks pass. For $80, the pass will provide admission to any national park for a full year. You're 62 or older? Even better—the cost drops to $10! How far will your money go? As far as 80.7 million acres of park land at 379 national parks, from Acadia in Maine to Zion in Utah, all cared for and explained by more than 20,000 rangers, archaeologists, historians, biologists, architects, laborers, and gardeners.

Food Faves

One of my favorite vocations while riding is finding great roadside diners along the highway or in a village. Two of my favorite American writers are Jane and Michael Stern, who, in addition to writing the classic *Elvis World*, wrote *Eat Your Way Across the USA: 500 Diners, Lobster Shacks, Buffets, Pie Palaces, and Other All-American Eateries.* While my book can lead you to a handful of restaurants, their book is a buffet of great American greasy spoons, hash houses, doughnut shops, cafeterias, and small-town cafés.

Offbeat USA

If your motivation to ride is partially fueled by the chance discovery of kitsch Americana, check out www.roadsideamerica.com. This site is the online guide to offbeat tourist attractions, and it may provide you with some side-trip ideas when you're in the vicinity of places like the Zippo Lighter Visitors Center in Bradford, PA, or the giant advertising statues that still plug businesses across the United States.

Selecting an Organized Tour

As the popularity of motorcycles grows, so does the proliferation of motorcycle tour operators. If you decide to ride on a prearranged trip, there are two constants you'll encounter: You will need a major credit card and a motorcycle endorsement on your license. There are also several variables. For instance, you may or may not need to bring your own bike, helmet, or rain gear.

With these variances, play it smart by asking the "stupid" questions. Ask who covers specific expenses: lodging, meals, tolls, fuel, laundry, tips, insurance. What type of lodging can you expect? Is it a flophouse, campground, or inn? Private bath? Shared rooms? Carrying a passenger will cost extra—how much? As you sift through these questions, also ask if you'll be allowed to break away from the group and meet them later. Is there a guide? A support vehicle? A trained mechanic? Does the ride include overnights, or do you return to the same city each evening?

Make sure that if your ride is cancelled because of inclement weather, your deposit will be refunded (you may want to safeguard your investment by taking out traveler's cancellation insurance).

CHAIN HOTEL GUIDE

Best Western
800/528-1234
www.bestwestern.com

Clarion
800/252-7466
www.choicehotels.com

Comfort Inn
800/221-2222
www.choicehotels.com

Courtyard by Marriott
800/321-2211
www.marriott.com

Days Inn
800/329-7466
www.daysinn.com

Doubletree
800/222-8733
www.doubletree.com

Econo Lodge
800/553-2666
www.choicehotels.com

Embassy Suites
800/362-2779
www.embassy-suites.com

Fairfield Inn
800/228-2800
www.fairfieldinn.com

Hampton Inn
800/426-7866
www.hampton-inn.com

Hilton
800/445-8667
www.hilton.com

Holiday Inn
800/465-4329
www.holiday-inn.com

Howard Johnson
800/446-4656
www.hojo.com

Hyatt
800/233-1234
www.hyatt.com

Knights Inn
800/843-5644
www.knightsinn.com

La Quinta
800/687-6667
www.laquinta.com

Motel 6
800/466-8356
www.motel6.com

Omni Hotels
800/843-6664
www.omnihotels.com

Quality Inn
800/228-5151
www.qualityinn.com

Radisson
800/333-3333
www.radisson.com

Ramada
800/272-6232
www.ramada.com

Red Carpet Inn
800/251-1962
www.reservahost.com

Red Roof Inn
800/843-7663
www.redroof.com

Residence Inn
800/331-3131
www.mariott.com

Rodeway
800/228-2000
www.rodewayinn.com

Scottish Inns
800/251-1962
www.reservahost.com

Sheraton
800/325-3535
www.sheraton.com

Sleep Inn
800/627-5337
www.sleepinn.com

Super 8
800/800-8000
www.super8.com

Travelodge
800/578-7878
www.travelodge.com

Acknowledgments

It's never far from my mind that an ongoing project like this requires assistance from others—and I've had it. There are hundreds of people across the nation who've pitched in to make this possible. As always, they're listed in order of their favorite Beatle.

John Lennon: John McKechnie, Bud McKechnie, Ian McKechnie, all McKechnies everywhere, Peter Fonda, Kevin McLain, Darren Alessi, Donna Galassi, Peg Goldstein, Cassandra Conyers, Dianna Delling, Robyn McPeters, Mike Zimmerman, Jennifer Gruber, Amanda Lee, Ty van Hooydonk, Michelle Greco, Joel Cliff, Walter Yeldell, Carrie Saldo, Beth Krauss, Ron Dusek, Jennifer Williams, Mary Ann McClain, Matthew Carinhas, Evelynn Bailey, David Lorenz, Amy Seng, Mike Norton, Andy Moon, Mike Houck, Dana Alley, George Milo, Ken Thompson, Jessica Icenhour, Fred Good, Jana Greenbaum, Chuck Haralson, Ken Grimsley, Lisa Richardson, Tracy Brown, Alissa Clark, Bill Seratt, Mary Beth Romig, Carl Whitehill, Anne Barney, Tessy Shirakawa, Bronwyn Patterson, Marci Penner, Kathy Giffin, Cindy Andrus, Chad Sterns, Dan Bookham, Valerie Ryan, Jimmy Sample, Jeff Feldman, Eden Umble, Celeste White, Heather Hermen, Walter Yeldell, Barbara Golden, Jennifer Haz, Erik Skindrud, Lou Ann Nelson, Heather Falk, David Fantle, Jon Jarosh, Jeri Riggs, Lynn Berry, Nick Noyes, Jo Sabel Courtney, John Formichella, Anne Marie Basher, Nancy Arena, Ruth Parsons, Stacey Fox, Philip Magaldi, Charles Hardin, Melody Heltman, Erika Backus, Rich Wittish, Chris Nobles, Melina Martinez, Michelle Revuelta, Josie Gulliksen, Emy Bullard Wilkinson, Beverly Gianna, Jon Jarosh, George Milos, Jezal McNeil, Phil Lampert, Kelly Barbello, Kim Latrielle, Judy Siring, Jay Humphries, Anne Barney, Sandy Smith, Kim Cobb....

Paul McCartney: Jean James, Lin Lee, Susan Albrecht, Patricia Kiderlen, Lynn Dyer, Judith Swain, Suzanne Elder, Phyllis Reller, Karen Baker, Gwen Peterson, Tony Fortier, Ken McNenny, Susan Sullivan, Pepper Massey-Swan, Karen Connelly, Liz Porter, Steve Lewis, Shelly Clark, Susie Haver, Jenny Stacy, Susan Belanski, Jack Dunlavy, Phillip Magdali Jr., Paula Tirrito, Steven Skavroneck, Valerie Parker, Joel Frey, Lenore Barkley, Jan Osterman, Howard

Gray, Christine DeCuir, Sandy Tucker, Don Sparks, DeRoy Jenson, Ed and Minna Williams, Rennie Ross, Didi Bushnell, Jim Pelletier, Stan Corneil, Chris Mackey, Amy Ballenger, Jeff Ehoodin, Jeff Webster, Nina Kelly, Todd Morgan, Dave Blanford, Nancy Borino, Tom Lyons, Krista Elias, Shannon Mackie-Albert, Carolyn Hackney, Rachel Keating, Maureen Oltrogge, Mike Finney, Julia Scott, Sue Bland, Natasha Johnston, Janie McCullough, Laura Simoes, Tessie Shirwakawa, Aimee Grove, Melanie Ryan, Steve Lewis, Jan Mellor, Jennifer Wess, Kathy Lambert, Dwayne Cassidy, Ron Terry, Erika Yowell, Kathleen New, Wyndham Lewis, Dennis Cianci, Marjie Wright, Karen Hamill, Sue Ellen Peck, Tom Hash, Rick Gunn....

George Harrison: Rick Wilder, Ken Crouse, Donna Bonnefin, Pettit Gilwee, Keith Walklet, Amy Herzog, Susan Carvalho, Kathy Langley, Kirk Komick, Jennifer Franklin, Mike Pitel, Jody Bernard, Sarah Pitcher, Nancy Brockman, Paul Schreiner, Bev Owens, Billy Dodd, Heather Deville, Sarah Baker, Joel Howard, Annie Kuehls, Bob and Paula Glass, Troy Duvall, Matt Bolas, Carrie Clark, Trey Hines, Tony Hayden, Chris Jones, Haley Gingles, Greg Lasiewski, Jan Plessner, Tim Buche, Cheryl Smith, Trish Taylor, Hal Williams, Emily Raabe, Cara O'Donnell, Alan Rosenzweig, Barbara Ashley, Janet Dutson, Mary Bennoch, Jeff Lupo, John and Diane Sheiry, Croft Long, Mel Moore, Mark Kayser, Lisa Umiker, Rich Gates, Ray Towells, Julie Smith, Scott Gediman, Mike Dorn, Wendy Haase, Jan Dorfler, Mary Cochran, Traci Varner, Dirk Oldenburg, Mark Reese, Scott Heath, Linda Adams....

Ringo Starr: Trevor and Regina Aldhurst, Rosemary and Fabrizio Chiarello, Frank and Mary Newton, Mary Beth Hutchinson, Anna Maria Dalton, Karen Hedelt, Emily Case, Pauli Galin, Carol Jones, Sue Mauro, Beth Culbertson, Ron Gardner, Ellen Gillespie, Timothy James Trifeletti, Carrie Wilkinson-Tuma, Elmer Thomas, Nancy and Tom Blackford, Karen Suffredini, Mike McGuinn, Susan Williams, Virginia Mure, Ron and Sue Ramage, Leslie Prevish and Joe Hice....

Pete Best: Every engineer, surveyor, road crew, and chain gang that helped build America's beautiful back roads.

About the Author

Gary Mckechnie

As an advertising copywriter, Gary McKechnie spent his days writing about how consumers could design a better life. Influenced by his own writing, he decided to design a better life for himself. He started by quitting his job.

The decision was in line with earlier steps Gary took to make sure that his life would be consistently interesting. He put himself through college as a stand-up comedian and skipper on Walt Disney World's Jungle Cruise. The morning after graduating, he didn't report to a new job—he hopped on a flight to Europe instead, the beginning of a seven-month backpacking and hitchhiking excursion across the continent.

Returning to the United States, Gary earned enough money through a series of short-term jobs to enjoy long-term travel. He began exploring America by motorcycle and by car, and eventually decided on a career that would subsidize his vacations: writing travel features for newspapers and magazines. In 2000, he completed the 20,000-mile motorcycle odyssey that resulted in the first edition of *Great American Motorcycle Tours*. It became the first motorcycle guidebook to receive two awards: the Lowell Thomas Travel Journalism Award (recognized as the Pulitzer Prize of travel writing) and the Benjamin Franklin Gold Award, presented by the Publisher's Marketing Association.

In addition to taking lengthy road trips for subsequent editions of *Great American Motorcycle Tours*, Gary conducted an intensive national tour to research the places, events, and festivals that collectively create the American Experience. The result of his efforts was his next book, *USA 101*, published in May 2009. It has been featured in local, regional, and national media, and is one of only two *National Geographic* travel publications recommended by the American Library Association's *Booklist*. In December 2009, Gary became a speaker for Cunard Insights, presenting his views on America aboard the *Queen Mary 2*.

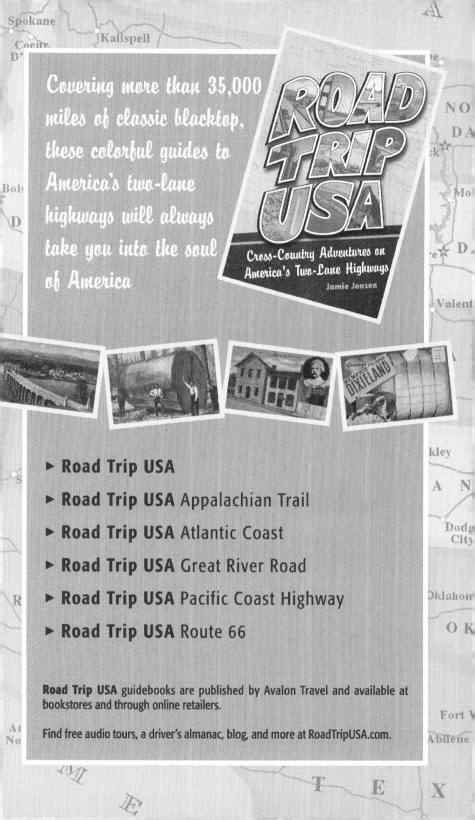

Great American
Motorcycle Tours of the Northeast
Avalon Travel
a member of the Perseus Books Group
1700 Fourth Street
Berkeley, CA 94710, USA

Editor: Kevin McLain
Copy Editor: Naomi Adler Dancis
Graphics and Production Coordinator:
  Darren Alessi
Cover and Interior Designer:
  Darren Alessi
Map Editor: Mike Morgenfeld
Cartographers: Kat Bennett, Brice Ticen

ISBN: 978-1-59880-584-0

Text © 2010 by Gary McKechnie.
Maps © 2010 by Avalon Travel.
All rights reserved.

Some photos and illustrations are used
by permission and are the property of the
original copyright owners.

Front cover photo: © Kenneth Sponsler/
  istockphoto.com
Title page photo: © Nancy Howell
All interior photos: © Nancy Howell

Printed in the United States

Made in the USA
Lexington, KY
19 May 2013